Make It Simple

メイク・イット・シンプル
基礎からの実践英語

Kazuko Morita / Junko Takahashi / Hiroko Kitamoto

SANSHUSHA

音声ダウンロード＆ストリーミングサービス（無料）のご案内

http://www.sanshusha.co.jp/onsei/isbn/9784384334463/

本書の音声データは、上記アドレスよりダウンロードおよびストリーミング再生ができます。ぜひご利用ください。

はじめに

　本書『Make It Simple（メイク・イット・シンプル—基礎からの実践英語—）』は、日常生活の中でよく目にしたり耳にしたりする英文素材を「読んだり」「聞いたり」できる力と、思ったことをシンプルな英語で「話したり」「書いたり」できる力をつけることを目指しています。

　本書は好評を頂いている『Communication in Simple English（発信型 シンプル・イングリッシュ）』の姉妹編・実践編で、前著同様、①身近な語彙の知識を増やし、②発信に必要な文法を確かなものにするという2つの基礎固めを大切に考えています。たくさんの練習問題を解く中で、しっかりとした土台を作ってください。

　また本書ではさらに、幅広いテーマでさまざまな素材に触れ、より実践的に英語を学べるように工夫しました。例えばキャンパス案内、アルバイトなどの大学在学中の生活に関する身近な話題のほかに、今回は就職・職場などの大学卒業後の生活に関する話題、さらには地図を広げての海外旅行など、近い将来みなさんが経験する可能性の高い場面を取り上げています。

　ところで本書のタイトル*Make It Simple*は、「あまり難しく考えないでシンプルに行こう！」という意味で、実はみなさんへの私達からのアドバイスです。さあ、肩の力を抜いて1ページ目を開けてみましょう。大学生のサトシや、先輩で社会人のケンタ、サヤカ夫妻など、個性的でどこかユーモラスな登場人物たちがみなさんを待っているはずです。

　最後になりましたが、Stephen Thompson氏には英文の校閲をお引き受け頂き、貴重な御助言を頂戴いたしました。ここに記して感謝申し上げます。

著　者

各課の構成

各課1つのテーマに沿って、以下の6種類の演習問題が展開します。

■ Let's Try

　ブログ、広告、オンラインショッピングのサイト、メール、案内状、キャンパスマップやチケットなど、シンプルな英語が実際に使われている生の素材に触れてみることから課をスタートさせましょう。最後のListening Check T/Fでは、内容が理解できたかどうかの確認を行います。

■ Words

　各課のテーマに関連した語句がイラストと一緒に出てきます。ピクチャー・ディクショナリーを使う気持ちで、楽しみながら語彙力を付けましょう。問題形式になっていますので、解答した後で声に出して練習してください。

■ Let's Listen

　各課のテーマに関連のある事柄についての聞き取りです。

■ Exercises

　文法問題です。問題を解きながら基礎的な文法の力を確かなものにしましょう。

■ Activities

　パートナーと会話して情報を交換します。

■ Let's Write

　その課で学んだことを生かして、自分で文を書いてみましょう。

Table of Contents

Lesson 1 家族 — 6
　Let's Try　ブログ　文法 be動詞①

Lesson 2 キャンパス案内 — 12
　Let's Try　キャンパスマップ　文法 be動詞②・場所の表現

Lesson 3 就職・職場 — 18
　Let's Try　1日のスケジュール表　文法 一般動詞①

Lesson 4 日課 — 24
　Let's Try　日記　文法 一般動詞②・代名詞

Lesson 5 交通 — 30
　Let's Try　転居通知　文法 命令文

Lesson 6 アルバイト — 36
　Let's Try　求人広告　文法 名詞を詳しく

Lesson 7 健康 — 42
　Let's Try　病院内の様子　文法 Wh疑問文①

Lesson 8 ショッピング — 48
　Let's Try　オンラインショッピングのサイト　文法 Wh疑問文②

Lesson 9 休日 — 54
　Let's Try　バスツアーのサイト　文法 時の表現

Lesson 10 大学生活 — 60
　Let's Try　メール　文法 助動詞

Lesson 11 世界の国々 — 66
　Let's Try　世界地図　文法 比較級と最上級

Lesson 12 海外旅行（1） — 72
　Let's Try　ヨーロッパ地図

Lesson 13 海外旅行（2） — 78
　Let's Try　チケット

Activities Student **B** のワークシート — 85

Lesson 1

家族
〔be 動詞①〕

Let's Try

サトシのブログです。記事と、記事に寄せられたコメントを読んでみましょう。

MY MOTORCYCLE, MY LIFE

March 20　Better part-time jobs
March 22　Judo Tournament
April 7　　I need more holidays
April 14　　I became an uncle

Profile

Name:	Satoshi
Hometown:	Yokohama
Job:	College student
Interests:	judo, motorcycles, traveling
Favorite Activities:	eating rice crackers and bitter chocolate, motorcycling along the seaside, playing computer games

20xx-04-14　22:45:38

I became an uncle

My sister gave birth to twins today: a boy and a girl! Congratulations to my sister! But is this good news for me? I am a twenty-year-old college student, and now I am Uncle Satoshi... How does that sound?

Comment 1 from **Baikichi**　20xx-04-15　19:12:29

Don't worry. I have a two-month-old aunt. My grandfather had a new wife and they had a baby-girl two months ago. Their daughter is, yes, my aunt! Think about my grandfather's new wife. She is only twenty-seven years old, but she is my grandmother-in-law. Can you believe it? Now my father has a very young sister. He is excited about it. Life is interesting!

Lesson 1　家族〔be動詞①〕

1　左のブログの内容と一致するものにT、しないものにFを記入しましょう。
1. サトシは丼物が好物である。　　　　　　　　　　　（　　）
2. サトシには双子の姉がいる。　　　　　　　　　　　（　　）
3. サトシは姉に子供が生まれて嬉しくてたまらない。　（　　）
4. バイキチさんのおじいさんは再婚して、2か月前に子供が生まれた。（　　）
5. バイキチさんには27歳の義理の伯母さんがいる。　　（　　）

2　ブログの内容に合うように、下から語句を選び、文章を完成させましょう。

Satoshi is (　　　　　) old. His (　　　　) and (　　　　　) were born on April 14th. They are his (　　　　)'s children.
Baikichi's (　　　　　　) married, and his new wife is (　　　　　) old. They had a (　　　　　) two months ago. Now, Baikichi has a very young (　　　) and a young grandmother.

> twenty-seven years / twenty years / daughter / aunt /
> grandfather / niece / sister / nephew

3　サトシについての質問です。答えを完成させましょう。
1. What is he?　　　　　　He _____
2. Where does he live?　　He _____
3. What is he interested in?　He _____
4. What are his favorite activities?　His favorite activities _____
　_____

4　上記の **3** を参考にして、あなたも自己紹介文を書いてみましょう。

_____
_____
_____

Listening Check! T / F　1〜4の音声を聞いて、ブログの内容に合っていればT、違っていればFを記入しましょう。

1.（　　　　） 2.（　　　　） 3.（　　　　） 4.（　　　　）

Words

家族関係

下は☺さんのFamily Treeです。1～12の人を表す語を右から選び、a～lで答えましょう。

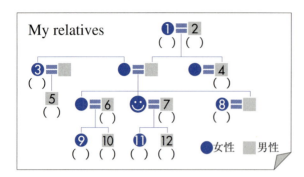

a. uncle　　b. aunt
c. daughter　d. son
e. husband　f. brother-in-law
g. sister-in-law
h. nephew　i. niece
j. cousin　　k. grandfather
l. grandmother

名詞と形容詞

1 (　)に当てはまる単語を下から選び書き入れましょう。

① shy /(　　) ② married /(　　) ③ polite /(　　) ④ clean /(　　)

⑤ quiet /(　　) ⑥ rich /(　　) ⑦ easygoing /(　　) ⑧ healthy /(　　)

⑨ great-grandfather /(　　) ⑩ thief /(　　) ⑪ husband /(　　) ⑫ employer /(　　)

| great-grandmother　policeman　dirty　single　employee |
| noisy　poor　serious　outgoing　rude　sick　wife |

2 上記 **1** の語を名詞と形容詞に分けてみましょう。

Let's Listen

1～7を聞いてTかFかを記入しましょう。

1.(　) **2.**(　) **3.**(　) **4.**(　) **5.**(　) **6.**(　) **7.**(　)

Lesson 1　家族〔be動詞①〕

Exercises

文法 be動詞を使うか、一般動詞を使うか

「〜は…だ」のようにイコールを表す文にはbe動詞を使い、「〜は…する」のように動作を表す場合には一般動詞を使います。

1 次の文はbe動詞と一般動詞のどちらを使いますか。「be」あるいは「一般」と記入しなさい。

1. (　　　) きのうサトシに会ったよ。
2. (　　　) あの人誰？
3. (　　　) この教科むずかしいよ。
4. (　　　) この電車、横浜に止まりますか？
5. (　　　) 僕は朝ごはんは食べない。
6. (　　　) いやあ、先週は忙しかったなあ。

文法 be動詞の語順パターン

下の図はbe動詞を使った文の語順パターンです。イコールの右辺が「なに」を表す場合には名詞がきて、「どんな」を表す場合には形容詞がきます。

①主語	②＝	③なに／どんな	
① Satoshi's brother-in-law	② is	③ a firefighter.	なに（名詞）
① He	② is	③ shy.	どんな（形容詞）

疑問文ではbe動詞が文の最初にきます。　Is　he　　　shy?
否定文ではbe動詞にnotがつきます。　　　He　is not　shy.

2 次の文の主語を○で囲み、be動詞に下線を引きなさい。また、上図の③に当たる語句が名詞と形容詞のどちらなのか(　　)に記入しなさい。

1. Sendai is my hometown.　(　　　　)
2. Am I late?　(　　　　)
3. My favorite sports are swimming and tennis.　(　　　　)
4. Were your parents childhood friends?　(　　　　)

3 次の語句は、上の図の「①主語」、「②＝」、「③なに／どんな」のどの場所に来ることができますか？(　　)に可能な番号をすべて書きなさい。

(　) your cousin　　　(　) cheap　　　(　) these books　　　(　) are
(　) careful　　　　 (　) is　　　　 (　) shy　　　　　　 (　) that tall man
(　) my grandchildren (　) easy　　　 (　) were　　　　　 (　) was
(　) this ring　　　 (　) my old friend (　) single　　　 (　) sick

4 上記 **3** の語句を使って2つ文を作りなさい。

5 例にならって2つの絵を説明しなさい。

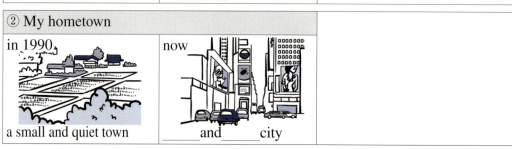

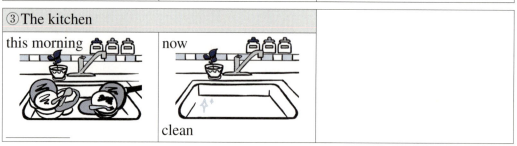

6 日本語の意味に合うように単語を並べ替えなさい。

1. 私の親戚はのんきで、とても健康です。
   (easygoing   my relatives   and   very   healthy   are).

2. あなたのひいおじいさんは中学校の先生だったのですか？
   (your great-grandfather   a junior high school teacher   was)?

3. 娘の新しいボーイフレンドのヨースケ君はとても礼儀正しい人です。
   (very   is   Yosuke   my daughter's new boyfriend   polite).

Lesson 1　家族〔be 動詞①〕

Activities　Student A

Student B ▶ p. 85

(1) あなたのパートナーは、あなたの家族・親戚について知りたがっています。下のFamily Treeについて、Bさんの質問に答えましょう。

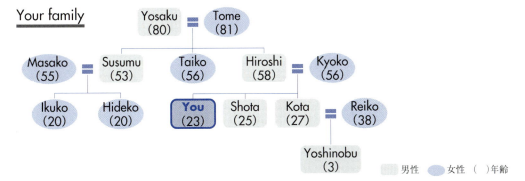

(2) 今度は、あなたがパートナーの家族・親戚について質問する番です。下のFamily TreeはBさんのものです。下の質問例を参考にして、右の6人の年齢は何歳なのか、パートナーとはどんな関係なのかを質問し、BさんのFamily Treeを完成させましょう。

　　質問例　・年齢を尋ねる場合…How old is Ume?
　　　　　・関係を尋ねる場合…Is she your aunt?（Who is she? と尋ねてはいけません。）

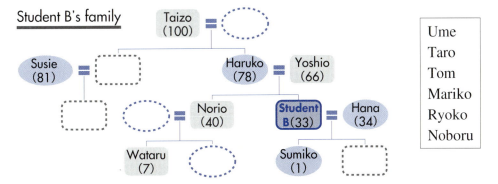

Ume
Taro
Tom
Mariko
Ryoko
Noboru

Let's Write

あなた自身が右のプロフィールをもつ人物だと仮定して想像力を働かせ、自己紹介する文章を書きましょう。

Name: Takuya	
Hometown: Kawasaki	Job: Actor
Interests: photography, surfing, playing the guitar	
Favorite Activities: cooking curry and rice, eating strawberries, watching the sunset on the beach, listening to music	

Lesson 2

キャンパス案内
〔be動詞②・場所の表現〕

Let's Try

サトシが大学のキャンパスを案内しています。地図を見ながら、説明文を読みましょう。

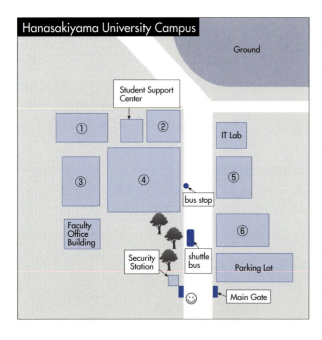

This is Hanasakiyama University. I am at the main gate now. Come in and see the campus!

The first building on the right is <u>Hanasaki Hall</u>. Its name comes from the founder* of the university. The entrance ceremonies, graduation ceremonies and other events are held here.

The <u>main building</u> is on the left. There is a bus stop in front of the main building. The shuttle bus runs between the campus and Haruyama Station. Here comes the bus! It's full of students.

The building across from the main building is the <u>library</u>. I borrow judo magazines there. I am the captain of the judo club and we practice in the <u>gym</u>. The gym is next to the main building. We usually practice three times a week, but before a tournament, we practice every day. Last year we won the spring championship!

There is a small building between the gym and the <u>dormitory</u>. We call that building the student support center. The health clinic is on the second floor of the building and the campus store is on the third floor. At the campus store, we can buy not only books, magazines and stationery, but also snacks and soft drinks.

Behind the main building is the <u>university cafeteria</u>. Cheerful cooks serve delicious meals. My favorite is the special lunch. I enjoy meat, fish and vegetables on a plate with steaming rice in a large rice bowl!

*founder 創設者

Lesson 2 キャンパス案内〔be動詞②・場所の表現〕

1 次の建物は、地図中①～⑥のどれでしょう。

Hanasaki Hall（　　　）　　　main building（　　　）
library（　　　）　　　gym（　　　）
dormitory（　　　）　　　university cafeteria（　　　）

2 次の質問に答えましょう。
1. 入学式、卒業式はどこで行われますか？
2. 柔道部の練習は週に何回ありますか？
3. 大学の教員がいる建物の名称は何でしょうか？　地図から捜しなさい。
4. コンピュータがたくさんある施設の名称は何でしょうか？　地図から捜しなさい。

3 次の質問に英語で答えましょう。
1. Where is Satoshi?　　He _____
2. Is the bus stop in front of the gym?
   _____
3. Is the health clinic on the first floor of the main building?
   _____
4. Where are you now? _____

4 次の和文の意味をあらわす英文を本文から書き抜きましょう。
1. 僕は正門のところにいます。　_____
2. 本館は左側です。　_____
3. 体育館は本館の隣にあります。　_____
4. 購買部は3階です。　_____

5 次の文中の____部分を日本語にしてみましょう。
1. The first building on the right is Hanasaki Hall.

2. The building across from the main building is the library.

Listening Check! T / F　　1～4の音声を聞いて、説明文の内容に合っていればT、違っていればFを記入しましょう。

1.（　　　）　2.（　　　）　3.（　　　）　4.（　　　）

Words

基本的な場所の前置詞

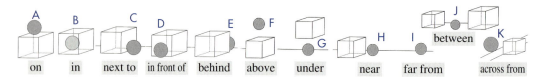

次のイラストの内容に合うように、適切な前置詞を下線部に書き入れ、文を完成させましょう。

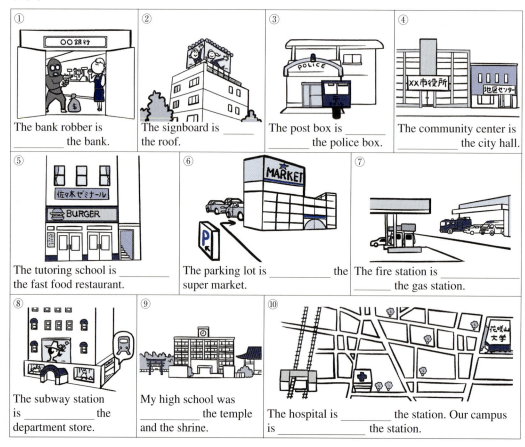

① The bank robber is _____ the bank.
② The signboard is _____ the roof.
③ The post box is _____ the police box.
④ The community center is _____ the city hall.
⑤ The tutoring school is _____ the fast food restaurant.
⑥ The parking lot is _____ the super market.
⑦ The fire station is _____ the gas station.
⑧ The subway station is _____ the department store.
⑨ My high school was _____ the temple and the shrine.
⑩ The hospital is _____ the station. Our campus is _____ the station.

Let's Listen

教卓				
ユカ	ケイコ	タロウ	ミドリ	ケン
コウタ	カズヤ	ナナ	ヒロシ	セイヤ
スミレ	フミヤ	シゲル	ヤスコ	サチ
エミ	アヤ	アキラ	ユウタ	カナエ

1～5の学生の座席についての説明を聞き、TかFかを記入しましょう。

1. ナナ　（　　）
2. セイヤ　（　　）
3. フミヤ　（　　）
4. ヒロシ　（　　）
5. ユウタ　（　　）

Lesson 2 キャンパス案内〔be動詞②・場所の表現〕

Exercises

文法 be動詞の語順パターン

下の図はbe動詞を使った文の語順パターンです。イコールの右辺が「どこ」を表す場合には前置詞句がきます。

主語	=	どこ
The security station	is	next to the main gate.
The cheer leaders	are	on the football field.

1 下の絵は、佐藤教授の研究室とその内部の様子です。いろいろなものの位置を英語で書きなさい。

例) The scissors are in the first drawer.

1. _____
2. _____
3. _____
4. _____
5. _____
6. _____
7. _____

ヒント　Professor Sato's office / stapler / stick of glue / scotch tape / flower pot / pen stand / calendar / umbrella

文法 名詞を詳しく

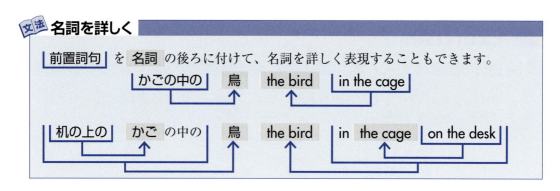

2 次の文の主語を○で囲み、be動詞に下線を引きなさい。
1. The building is on the hill.
2. The building on the hill is our university.
3. Were the clerks at the career center helpful?

3 次の日本語に合うように語句を並べ替えなさい。
1. (写真を見せながら)真ん中にいる男の子が僕のいとこだよ。
   (middle   in   the boy   my   is   the   cousin).

2. 私の後ろの男の子たちがうるさくて、先生の声が聞こえなかった。
   (me   behind   the boys   noisy   were), so I couldn't hear my teacher.

3. バイキチ君は今日の授業に出てたかな？
   (Baikichi   today   was   class   in)?

4 英語にしなさい。
1. バス停はここから遠いですか？

2. 右手にある背の高い建物は六本木ヒルズです。

3. 私の車はスーパーの裏の駐車場です。

Lesson 2　キャンパス案内〔be動詞②・場所の表現〕

■ Activities　Student A

Student B ▶ p. 86

（1）次の写真に写っている人たちは誰なのか、例にならってパートナーに説明しましょう。

例）The woman next to me is my mother.

（2）次の写真に写っている人たちは誰なのか、パートナーの説明を聞いて日本語で写真に書き込みましょう。

■ Let's Write

あなたの大学には次の施設や設備がありますか？　3つ以上選んで、どこにあるかを英語で書きなさい。

a. cafeteria　　　　b. ground　　　　c. tennis court
d. computer room　e. health clinic　f. gym　　　　g. campus store
h. security station　i. parking lot　　j. career center

Lesson 3

就職・職場
〔一般動詞①〕

Let's Try

鈴木ケンタ・サヤカ夫妻は柔道部のOBです。いつもの1日の様子を、ケンタが話しています。

"I work at an insurance company, and Sayaka works as a chef at a small Italian restaurant, *Milano*. Our typical day goes like this."

Time	Kenta	Sayaka
7:00		Sayaka drives to the market.
9:00	I ( ) the train to work.	She ( ) some vegetables, meat and fish.
	I ( ) my schedule for today.	She takes out the garbage at *Milano*.
	I prepare documents on my P.C.	She ( ) today's menu on the blackboard.
11:00	I ( ) a presentation at the meeting.	She ( ) brunch with her co-workers.
12:00	I ( ) with the customers on the phone.	She ( ) *Milano*.
	I skip the meeting... sometimes.	She ( ) pizza and other Italian dishes.
	I ( ) the deadline and apologize* to my boss.	She ( ) the dishes.
9:00	I ( ) overtime.	She hangs the "Closed" plate on the door.
10:00	I ( ) to a ramen shop, Chinraiken.	She ( ) to a ramen shop, Chinraiken.
10:30	Sayaka and I eat ramen. We go home by car.	

*apologize 謝る

Lesson 3　就職・職場〔一般動詞①〕

1 左ページの（ ）にはどんな動詞が入るでしょうか。下の□から語を選び、適切な形にして入れましょう。

Kenta				Sayaka				
miss	talk	hurry	take	make	hurry	dry	buy	open
work	check	make		have	write			

2 自分の仕事についての思いを、ケンタとサヤカが次のように話してくれました。この2人の話と左ページの表を読んで、下の1～9が合っていればT、違っていればFを記入しましょう。

Well, actually, I don't like my job very much. The pay is good, but the job is hard. I work overtime almost every day. Besides, I hate paper working. I like talking with people better than sitting at a desk. I am looking for a new job. What do you think about a tutoring school teacher or a fitness instructor?

Kenta

Sayaka

I like my job. I like cooking and I feel happy when I see the customers having a good time in the restaurant. Of course the job is hard. I leave home very early and work until late at night, but I still love my job.

1. ケンタはサヤカよりも早く家を出る。　　　　　　　　　（　　）
2. ケンタは行き帰りとも電車を使う。　　　　　　　　　　（　　）
3. サヤカは市場で仕入れをしてから店に行く。　　　　　　（　　）
4. レストラン・ミラノはサヤカひとりに任されていて、他に従業員はいない。（　　）
5. ケンタは締め切りだけは絶対に守るようにしている。　　（　　）
6. 2人は珍来軒で待ち合わせをして、一緒に帰る。　　　　（　　）
7. ケンタもサヤカも給料に不満を持っている。　　　　　　（　　）
8. ケンタはデスクワークよりも人と接する仕事が自分には向いていると考えている。　　　　　　　　　　　　　　　　　　　　　　　　（　　）
9. サヤカは朝ゆっくり出勤できて夜も遅くならないような仕事を探している。（　　）

Listening Check! T / F　1～4の音声を聞いて、内容に合っていればT、違っていればFを記入しましょう。

1. (　　　)　2. (　　　)　3. (　　　)　4. (　　　)

Words

職　業

A〜Jの職業を下から選んで番号を書きましょう。

A(　)　B(　)　C(　)　D(　)　E(　)
F(　)　G(　)　H(　)　I(　)　J(　)

①　dental hygienist　②　dietitian　③　care worker　④　hairdresser
⑤　kindergarten teacher　⑥　sales assistant　⑦　tutoring school teacher
⑧　pharmacist　⑨　architect　⑩　lawyer

就　職

英語で何と言うのでしょう。下から選びなさい。

給料(　)　会議(　)　上司(　)　書類(　)　履歴書(　)
就職活動(　)　就職の面接(　)　〜に応募する(　)　残業する(　)
1日休暇をとる(　)　プレゼンをする(　)　出張で〜に行く(　)
仕事を辞める(　)　職を失う(　)　クビにする(　)

①　meeting　②　quit the job　③　resume　④　fire　⑤　pay　⑥　make a presentation
⑦　go to 〜 on business　⑧　take a day off　⑨　lose the job　⑩　apply for 〜
⑪　document　⑫　job hunting　⑬　boss　⑭　job interview　⑮　work overtime

Let's Listen

電話番号を聞き取りましょう。電話番号は2回読み上げられます。

営業部	Sales Department	(　) - (　) - (　)
マーケティング部	Marketing Department	(　) - (　) - (　)
設計部	Design Department	(　) - (　) - (　)
顧客サービス部	Customer Service Department	(　) - (　) - (　)
広告/広報部	Advertising Department	(　) - (　) - (　)
アイティー部	I.T. (Information Technology) Department	(　) - (　) - (　)
東京本社	Tokyo Head Office	(　) - (　) - (　)
福岡支社	Fukuoka Branch	(　) - (　) - (　)

Lesson 3 就職・職場〔一般動詞①〕

Exercises

一般動詞の語順パターン

下の図は一般動詞を使った文の語順パターンです。主語と目的語には名詞句がきます。

①主語	②一般動詞	③目的語	④その他（いつ・どこで・どのように）
① My boss	② drinks	③ strong coffee	④ at his desk　　　after lunch.
① The young men	② work	×	④ at the trading company.

1 「明日のスケジュールは私があとで確認しておきます」を英語でいうとき、「明日のスケジュール」「私」「あとで」「確認する」は、上図の①〜④のどこに入りますか。日本語で書きなさい。

①	②	③	④

2 主語を○で囲み、一般動詞に下線 ＿＿ を引き、目的語を □ で囲みなさい。

1. I sent my resume to a food company last month.

2. The meeting starts at 9:00 a.m.

3. My boss goes to the Fukuoka branch every Tuesday.

4. Our company makes computer programs.

3 次の語句は、上図の「①主語」「②一般動詞」「③目的語」「④その他」のどの場所に来ることができますか。（　）に可能な番号をすべて書きなさい。

(　) your boss　　(　) on Wednesday　　(　) she　　(　) you
(　) her　　(　) them　　(　) Yuki and Satoshi　　(　) came
(　) have　　(　) the big turtle　　(　) it　　(　) reads
(　) in the bag　　(　) me　　(　) in the morning　　(　) quickly
(　) put　　(　) the documents　　(　) to the company　　(　) brings

4 上の **3** の語句を使って2つ文を作りなさい。

5 例にならって①〜⑤の人たちの職業を紹介し、「どこで」「何を」「どうしている」のかも書きなさい。

例	Ms. Sato	is	a lawyer.
①			
②			
③			
④			
⑤			

She	makes	legal advice	at the office.

| sell | give | serve | | clothes | teeth | haircuts |
| clean | make | grow | | legal advice | food | rice |

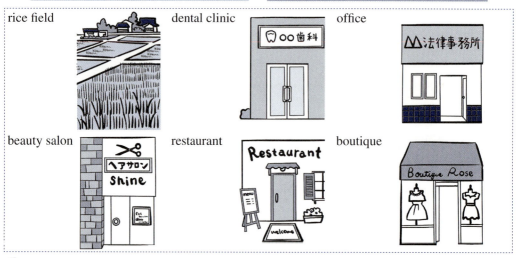

6 英語にしなさい。

1. 毎週火曜日は大事な会議があります。

2. 兄は設計部で車をデザインしています。

Lesson 3　就職・職場〔一般動詞①〕

■ Activities　Student A

Student B ▶ p. 87

（1）あなたは「カネマス銀行　顧客サービス部」に勤務しています。鈴木ケンタさんの名刺（business card）を参考にして、あなたの名刺を作ってみましょう。住所欄にはあなたの大学の住所を書くことにします。

All Star Insurance Company
Kenta Suzuki
Sales Dept.

Minato Bldg. 1-x-x Jingumae, Shibuya-ku
Tokyo 150-0001 Japan　Phone: +81-3-9876-1234

（2）下は鈴木ケンタさんが名刺交換したときの挨拶です。これを参考にしてパートナーと名刺交換の挨拶をし、パートナーの名前、勤務先、所属部を聞き取りましょう。

Kenta

Hello. My name is Kenta Suzuki. Nice to meet you.
I work for All Star Insurance Company. I'm in the Sales Department.

名前（　　　　　　　　　）勤務先（　　　　　　　　　　　）所属（　　　　　　　　　）

■ Let's Write

社長秘書の片野つき子さんのデスクです。片野さんはふだんどんなことをしているのか、絵から読み取って英文で書いてみましょう。

ヒント　phone calls / the schedule / send / arrange

Lesson 4

日課
〔一般動詞②・代名詞〕

Let's Try

次の2人が書いた日記を読みましょう。

Satoshi's Diary

Today was a terrible day.

I got up very early this morning, because I was so excited about meeting a girl at 10:00 a.m. We met at a party last night and made a date to go to see a movie in Shibuya. I took a shower, got dressed, and left home. I arrived in Shibuya at about 9:30 a.m. At about 10:00 a.m., I saw a girl with long curly hair. I thought it was her, but I was wrong. After waiting for another 30 minutes, a woman in a red coat passed in front of me, but again it was not her. I was worried, and sent her a message: HI! I ARRIVED. TAKE YOUR TIME. I waited and waited but there was no reply*. It was almost 12:00 p.m. I was very worried, so I sent her another message: I'M WAITING. BE CAREFUL ON YOUR WAY HERE. This time I received an e-mail: THIS ADDRESS IS NO LONGER BEING USED. I cannot believe it! Today was the most unlucky day of my life.

*reply 返信

Sachiko's Diary

I went to a party last night. It was fun, but maybe I drank too much. This morning I was very sleepy and had a terrible headache. I didn't remember anything about the party. I just couldn't get up, so I stayed home in bed. At about 10:30 a.m., I received an e-mail from a stranger. Junk mail* again. I changed my e-mail address, and went back to sleep.

*junk mail 迷惑メール

Lesson 4　日課〔一般動詞②・代名詞〕

1 次の文章は、サトシとサチコの日記の内容から2人に起こった出来事をまとめたものです。文中の下線を引いた語句に相当する英語を左の日記文の中から書きぬきましょう。

サトシとサチコは昨日、(1)パーティーで出会いました。そこでメールアドレスを交換し、翌日に渋谷で映画を見に行く(2)約束をしました。嬉しくてたまらないサトシは朝早く起きて、30分も前に約束の場所に着き、サチコを待ちましたが、彼女は現れません。髪の長い女性や赤いコートを着た女性を見かけますが、彼女ではありませんでした。心配になって(3)サチコにメールを送りましたが、一方のサチコは、昨日のパーティーで(4)お酒を飲み過ぎてしまって、頭痛でアパートで寝ています。パーティーのことは何もおぼえていないサチコはサトシから(5)メールを受け取りますが、迷惑メールだと思い、(6)アドレスを変更してしまいました。サトシにとっては最悪の1日でした。

(1) _____
(2) _____
(3) _____
(4) _____
(5) _____
(6) _____

2 正しい答えを選びましょう。

1. What did Satoshi do before he got dressed?
   He (took a shower / left home / went to see a movie).

2. Did a woman in a red coat pass by at about 10:30?
   (Yes, she did. / No, she didn't).

3. How many e-mails did he send to Sachiko?
   He sent (one / two / three) e-mails.

4. How long did Satoshi wait for her?
   He waited for about (thirty minutes / two hours / two and a half hours).

Listening Check! T / F 1～4の音声を聞いて、日記の内容に合っていればT、違っていればFを記入しましょう。

1. (　　　)　2. (　　　)　3. (　　　)　4. (　　　)

Words

日常の行動

1 下の英語表現はイラスト①〜⑱のどの行動を表していますか。（ ）に番号を入れましょう。

( ) shave myself
( ) take a shower
( ) wash my face
( ) chat with my friends
( ) wait for the bus
( ) hurry to my part-time job

( ) serve the dishes
( ) get up
( ) take a nap
( ) leave home
( ) have lunch at the cafeteria
( ) greet my neighbors

( ) listen to the lecture
( ) attend judo practice
( ) brush my teeth
( ) play hide and seek
( ) come home
( ) go to bed

2 上の①〜⑱ の表現を過去形にして言ってみましょう。

Let's Listen

雑誌記者が有名な映画スターに休日の過ごし方について質問しています。インタビューをよく聞き、このスターの回答に含まれる行動をリストから選びましょう。

☐ put on make-up
☐ play computer games
☐ do the laundry
☐ cook breakfast
☐ take out the garbage
☐ do yoga
☐ wash his face
☐ go shopping

Lesson 4　日課〔一般動詞②・代名詞〕

Exercises

文法 一般動詞の疑問文・否定文

疑問文	Do	you	make	breakfast ?
否定文		You	don't + make	breakfast .

主語が3人称単数の場合は<u>does</u>を用います。（次ページの図の網掛け部参照）
過去形の場合は、主語の人称にかかわらず<u>did</u>を用います。

1 次の文を疑問文、または否定文に書き換えなさい。

1. She puts on make-up on Sundays.（否定文に）

   _____

2. Mr. Tanaka takes out the garbage when his wife is busy.（疑問文に）

   _____

3. He left home early this morning.（否定文に）

   _____

4. Yuki does the laundry for her mother.（疑問文に）

   _____

5. Satoshi did his homework last night.（否定文に）

   _____

2 次の文の主語を○で囲み、一般動詞に＿＿を引き、目的語があれば□で囲みなさい。

1. Yuki dried her hair with a bath towel in front of the mirror.

2. Did all the trains and buses stop last night?

3. Does Professor Sato come to school on Mondays?

3 （　）に適語を入れ、文を完成させなさい。

1. My father is a vegetarian. He (　　　　　) eat meat or fish.

2. I was sleepy, so I (　　　　　) a nap.

3. You look pale. (　　　　　) you sick?

4. It (　　　　　) cold yesterday, but I (　　　　　) put on my coat.

27

4 間違いを直しなさい。

1. Are your grandfather jog every day?

2. He didn't made breakfast this morning. He buy sandwiches at the convenience store.

3. Were you cook lunch yesterday?

《代名詞》

5 名詞と代名詞の表です。表の（ ）には下から語句を選んで番号を書き入れ、〈 〉には代名詞を書きなさい。

				主語の時	所有「〜の」	目的語の時
1人称	単数		私	I	my	me
	複数	（ ）（ ）… ⇒私たち		we	〈 　 〉	〈 　 〉
2人称	単数		あなた	you	〈 　 〉	you
	複数	（ ）（ ）… ⇒あなたたち		〈 　 〉	〈 　 〉	you
3人称	単数	人間	（ ）（ ）… ⇒彼	he	〈 　 〉	〈 　 〉
			（ ）（ ）… ⇒彼女	〈 　 〉	〈 　 〉	〈 　 〉
		もの	（ ）（ ）… ⇒それ	it	〈 　 〉	it
	複数	人間	（ ）（ ）… ⇒彼ら	〈 　 〉	〈 　 〉	〈 　 〉
		もの	（ ）（ ）… ⇒それら			

① these cards　　② you and your brother　　③ Kenta
④ Mr. and Mrs. Kato　　⑤ our new car　　⑥ you and I
⑦ that tall girl　　⑧ her new earrings　　⑨ their sister
⑩ money　　⑪ my classmates　　⑫ you and Satoshi
⑬ my uncle　　⑭ Yuki and I

6 （　）に代名詞を入れなさい。

1. Satoshi bought a new mobile phone, and he likes (　　　) very much.
2. Sayaka and Yuka work at the same restaurant. (　　　) are rivals.
3. Ms. Sato has twins. She takes (　　　) to the park every day.
4. Kenta and I visited his uncle in Kyoto. He showed (　　　) around the city.
5. Yuki and I are classmates. (　　　) have lunch together every day.
6. Ms. Kato went snowboarding, and broke (　　　) right leg.

Activities Student A

Student B ▶ p. 88

Lesson 4 日課〔一般動詞②・代名詞〕

(1) 次のTo Do Listは昨日のBさんの手帳に書かれていたものです。Bさんに、実際にこれらのことをやったのかどうか、ひとつひとつ質問し、やったことには✓をつけましょう。やらなかったことについては、その理由を尋ね、表に日本語で記入しなさい。

B's To Do List

☐ get a haircut	
☐ make a reservation for concert tickets	
☐ contact the coach	
☐ buy a train pass	
☐ pay the phone bill	
☐ clean my room	
☐ do my English homework	

(2) 今度は、あなたの昨日のTo Do Listについて、Bさんの質問に英語で答えてみましょう。

Your To Do List

☐静岡のおばあちゃんと電話で話す	彼女は電話に出なかった（not / answer / the phone）
☑図書館に本を返す	
☐歯医者に行く	保険証を失くした（lose / insurance card）
☑田中先生に会いに行く	
☐洗濯をする	洗濯洗剤（laundry detergent）がなかった
☑リクルートスーツを買う	
☐ゴミ出しをする	さぼった（lazy）

Let's Write

あなた自身のことについて、きのう1日の行動を英語で書いてみましょう。10個以上書くこと。

Lesson 5

交通
〔命令文〕

■ Let's Try

サトシは、先輩のケンタ・サヤカ夫妻から次のような案内状をもらい、喜んで出かけました。

Invitation to a Housewarming Party

We have moved to our new apartment.
We would be happy if you could join us for a housewarming party.

Date: Sunday, June 6   **Time**: 4:00 p.m. ~
Address: 56-x-203 Hirose-cho, Atsugi-shi, Kanagawa   243-8501
Phone: 080-9876-5432 (Kenta) 080-8765-4321 (Sayaka)

Directions to our apartment

Take the Odakyu Line, and get off at Atsugi Station. (Express doesn't stop at Atsugi. Take the local train.) Use the West Exit. Take the No.4 bus and get off at the Keyakidai bus stop. From the bus stop, use the map below to get to our house. If you have any trouble, give us a call. We're looking forward to seeing you.

Sayaka & Kenta Suzuki

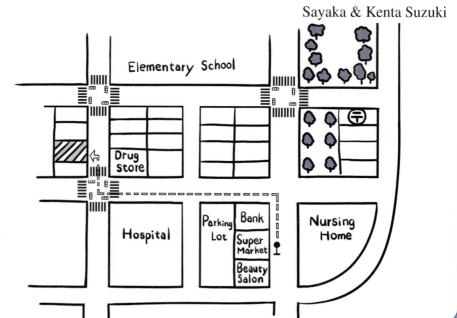

Lesson 5　交通〔命令文〕

1 内容に合っていればTを、合わなければFを記入しましょう。
1. これは6月6日（日）の午後4時から行われる新居引っ越し祝いの案内状である。（　　）
2. ケンタ先輩は電車の駅から自宅までのルートを地図に書いてくれた。（　　）
3. ケンタ先輩の家に行くには急行電車が便利である。（　　）
4. ケンタ先輩の家に行くには駅の西口からバスに乗ればよい。（　　）
5. バスを降りたら電話をかけることになっている。（　　）

2 当日電車に乗ってからバスを降りるまでのサトシの行動を、英語で書いてみましょう。

He took the Odakyu Line, _____

_____

_____

3 サトシはバスを降りてから道に迷い、ケンタ先輩に電話をします。下はそのときの電話の会話です。このあと、電話をかけた地点からアパートまでサトシはどのように歩いたのでしょう。左ページの地図に→で書き込みましょう。

Satoshi: Hello, Kenta-san. I think I'm lost.
Kenta: Have you got off the bus yet?
Satoshi: Yes. I'm now in front of the convenience store next to the post office.
Kenta: Oh, you have taken the wrong way. OK, Satoshi. Turn left at the post office. Go along the street. Turn left at the second traffic light. Our apartment building is the third building on the right. Hurry up! We are just about to make a toast*!

* toast 乾杯

4 バス停からアパートまでの道順（地図中の点線）を、もしあなたが説明するとしたら、どう言いますか。英語で書いてみましょう。

Turn _____

_____

_____

Listening Check! T / F　1〜4の音声が、左ページの地図に合っていればT、違っていればFを記入しましょう。

1.（　　　）　2.（　　　）　3.（　　　）　4.（　　　）

Words

街中

下の英語表現が表しているものをイラストから選び、（　）に番号を書き入れましょう。

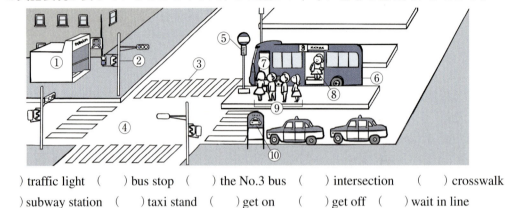

( ) traffic light　( ) bus stop　( ) the No.3 bus　( ) intersection　( ) crosswalk
( ) subway station　( ) taxi stand　( ) get on　( ) get off　( ) wait in line

動き・方向の前置詞

右から適切な前置詞を選んで（　）に入れましょう。

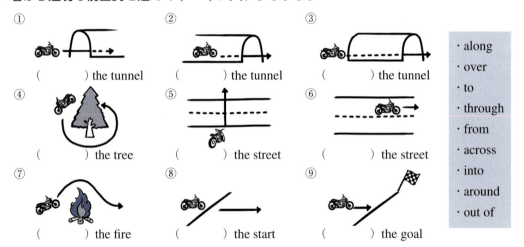

① (　) the tunnel　② (　) the tunnel　③ (　) the tunnel
④ (　) the tree　⑤ (　) the street　⑥ (　) the street
⑦ (　) the fire　⑧ (　) the start　⑨ (　) the goal

- along
- over
- to
- through
- from
- across
- into
- around
- out of

Let's Listen

空港でのアナウンスを聞いて、下の出発時刻表示板の（　）に数字を入れましょう。

Departures			
Flight Number	Destination	Departure Time	Gate Number
UA ( )	San Francisco	12：40	( )
AC 146	Toronto	( )	( )
JL ( )	Narita	( )	12
PA ( )	Manila	13：15	( )
BA ( )	London Heathrow	13：20	( )

Lesson 5 　交通〔命令文〕

Exercises

文法 命令文

命令文は主語を省略して原形動詞から始めます。
否定文は一般動詞も be 動詞も Don't ＋原形動詞です。

	一般動詞			be 動詞		
	You	change	trains.	You	are	ambitious.
命令文		Change	trains.		Be	ambitious.
否定の命令文	Don't	change	trains.	Don't	be	ambitious.

1 BさんはAさんにどう答えたのでしょう。（　　）内の語を並べ替えなさい。ただし余分な語が1つあります。

1. A: A big earthquake is happening!　B: (the table / getting / under / get).
   _____

2. A: This new computer doesn't work.　B: (the shop / to / doesn't / return / it).
   _____

3. A: I have lost my ATM card.　　　　B: (the bank / me / now / call).
   _____

4. A: I have a toothache.　　　　　　　B: (to / don't / a dentist / go).
   _____

2 おじいちゃんの100歳の記念撮影をしようとしています。カメラマンは下の1～9の注意を誰に向かって与えればよいのでしょう。（　　）にA～Jを入れなさい。

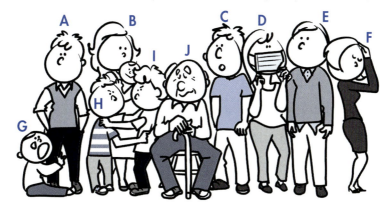

1. Don't open your mouth. (　　)
2. Look at the camera and smile. (　　)
3. Don't put your hands in your pockets. (　　)
4. Don't cry. (　　)
5. Take off your surgical mask. (　　)
6. Don't fight. Be good. (　　)(　　)
7. Move a little to the right. (　　)
8. Don't fall asleep. Open your eyes. (　　)
9. Your shirt is hanging out of your pants. Tuck your shirt into your pants. (　　)
10. Make happy faces. Say, "Cheese!" (Everyone)

3 (　)の語を使って英語にしなさい。

1. 神経質になっちゃだめだよ。(nervous)　リラックスしなさい！

2. 心配しないで。(worry)　私は大丈夫。

4 (　)には動詞を、＿＿＿には前置詞を、それぞれ □ から選んで書き入れ、切符を買ってから電車に乗るまでの動作を説明しなさい。

1. Look at the map _____ the ticket vending machine.

2. (　　　) the price.

3. (　　　) the money into the ticket vending machine.

4. (　　　) the button with your fare*.

5. (　　　) your ticket and change*.

6. Put your ticket _____ the ticket gate*.

7. Walk _____ the ticket gate.

8. (　　　) for the train on the platform.

9. Get _____ the train.

*fare 運賃　*change おつり　*ticket gate 改札口

take　put　through　push　into　wait　find　on　above

動き・方向の前置詞

5 (　)にあてはまる前置詞をp. 32のWordsコーナーから選びなさい。

1. He took his key (　　　　　) his pocket, and locked the door.
2. I poured coffee (　　　) my cup, and added sugar and milk.
3. It is December twenty-first today. Christmas is just (　　　　) the corner.
4. How long does it take (　　　) Shinjuku (　　　) Harajuku?
5. The ball was rolling (　　　) the street and the car almost ran it over.
6. I saw an old man (　　　) the open door. He was lying in bed.
7. The horse jumped (　　　) the fence, and ran away.
8. They took a walk (　　　) the river.

Lesson 5 交通〔命令文〕

■ Activities Student A

Student B ▶ p. 89

（1）下は地下鉄の路線図です。下線部に適切な語を入れて、B駅からCafé Rの最寄り駅までの行きかたについての会話文を完成させましょう。

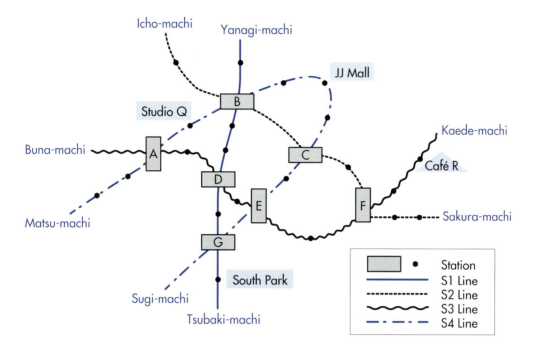

"Can you tell me how to get to Café R from Station B?"
"Sure. Take the _____ Line for Sakura-machi. Change trains at _____ . Take the _____ Line for _____ . Get off at the second stop. Café R is in front of the station."

（2）上の会話文を参考にしてパートナーに①〜③の行き方を質問し、説明に従って進んで、目的の施設を地図に書き込みましょう。
　　① D駅から Cinema X　　② F駅から Sky Tower　　③ G駅から K's Market

（3）今度はパートナーが質問してきます。路線図を見ながら答えましょう。

■ Let's Write

あなたの家にはどんなマナーやルールがありますか？　また、先生は学校でどんなマナーをみなさんに求めますか。
例）Come home by 10:00 p.m.　　Don't forget your textbook.

Lesson 6

アルバイト
〔名詞を詳しく〕

Let's Try

次の３つの求人広告 job ads を読みましょう。

Sushi Bar 三崎

A fancy sushi restaurant in Yokosuka is seeking a part-time delivery person. Hours: 7:00 p.m. – 12:00 a.m.（Friday & Saturday）
Wage: 54,000 yen/month（A mid-night supper is provided.*）
Requirements:* Applicants* must be 20 years or older and must have a valid motorcycle license.
For more information, call 030-1414-9191.

* provided 支給される　　* requirements 条件　　* applicants 応募者

Voice Actor or Actress

1-3-22 Nogizaka, Minato-ku

COMIC ACADEMIA is looking for a voice actor or actress. No experience* is necessary, but native English language skills are required.
Wage: 3,000 yen/hour＋transportation. Work hours are flexible.*
If you are interested, contact Mr. Bush at personnel@cacademia.com.

* experience 経験　　* flexible 融通が利く

Swimming Instructor

Stay Young Fitness since 1989

We're opening a new fitness center in Sugamo next autumn, and are looking to hire female swimming instructors. 3 positions are available.*
Requirements: No experience is necessary, but applicants must be good at communicating with elderly people. Wage: 1,200-1,600 yen/hour. Work days: negotiable*, but at least 2 days a week.
Visit our website for details: http://stay-young.com

*available 可　　*negotiable 応相談

Lesson 6　アルバイト〔名詞を詳しく〕

1　左の3つの求人広告の内容を下の表にまとめてみました。空欄を埋めましょう。

Company	Sushi Bar 三崎	Comic Academia	Stay Young Fitness
Job	delivery person	(　　　　　)	swimming instructor
Location	Yokosuka	(　　　　　)	Sugamo
Work days	(　　　　　)	flexible	(　　　　　)
Work hours	7:00 p.m.-12:00 a.m.	flexible	Not mentioned
Requirements	(　　　　　) (　　　　　)	(　　　　　)	ability to communicate with elderly people
Pay（¥）& other benefits	54,000 yen per month (　　　　　)	3,000 yen per hour + transportation	(　　　　　)
How to get information	telephone	(　　　　　)	website

2　求人の内容に合っていればTを、違っていればFを記入しましょう。
1. スイミングインストラクターの勤務日は相談で決められる。(　　　)
2. Stay Young Fitnessは男子のインストラクターを募集している。(　　　)
3. 声優の仕事は時給のほかに交通費が支給される。(　　　)
4. 寿司配達のバイトは昼食付である。(　　　)
5. スイミングインストラクターは月給制である。(　　　)

Listening Check! T / F　　1〜4の音声を聞いて、求人の内容に合っていればT、違っていればFを記入しましょう。

1.(　　　)　2.(　　　)　3.(　　　)　4.(　　　)

Words

アルバイト先

大学生のアルバイト先調査のグラフを見て、(　) に数字を入れましょう。

1. (　) percent of the interviewees work at fast food or other restaurants.
2. (　) percent are tutoring school teachers or private tutors.
3. (　) percent are clerks at convenience stores or supermarkets.
4. (　) percent don't have a part-time job.
5. (　) percent work as moving staff, delivery persons, movie extras, etc.

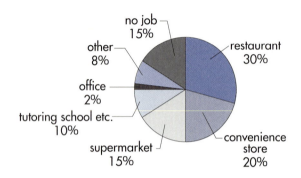

数字の読み方

アルバイト月収額のグラフを見て (　) に数字を入れ、下線の数字の読みを書きましょう。

11.5 %	38.5 %	14.8 %	25.1%	10.1%
~¥45,000	~¥60,000	~¥80,000	~¥110,000	¥110,000~

1. (　　　) % get less than ¥45,000 / month.

2. 10.1% get more than ¥ (　　　) per month.

3. (　　　) % get more than ¥60,000 and less than ¥110,000.

Let's Listen

A～Dの4つの数字をそれぞれ2回ずつ読み上げます。聞き取って (　) を埋めましょう。

	million			thousand					
A						7,	5	9	(　)
B				(　)	4	6,	0	(　)	2
C		(　)	2,	(　)	(　)	4,	8	0	(　)
D	(　)	7	0,	(　)	2	(　),	8	1	(　)

38

Lesson 6 アルバイト〔名詞を詳しく〕

Exercises

文法 名詞を詳しくする方法のまとめ

名詞を詳しく表現するには、次の3つの方法があります。
- ①前に形容詞などを付ける　　　　　a tall → girl
- ②後ろに前置詞句などを付ける　　　a　　girl ← with long hair
- ③上の①と②の組み合わせ　　　　　a tall → girl ← with long hair

1 次の日本語を表すように（　　）内の語を並べ替えなさい。

1. 静岡にいる私の親戚　（ Shizuoka / in / my / relatives ）

2. 仕事のない若者たち　（ jobs / without / people / young ）

3. ヴィトンのバッグを持ったあの女の人（a Luis Vuitton bag / woman / with / that ）

4. 勤務先の名前　（ your workplace / the / of / name）

2 サトシがバイト先の同僚の写真を見ながら話をしています。　　中の単語を並べ替えて、意味の通る文にしなさい。

There are many foreign students at my part-time workplace.

This _____ Muhammad.
　　　man / tall / a beard / with / is
He is from Iran.

The _____ Gandhi. He is from India.
　　　other / with / man / is / short hair

He doesn't speak Japanese well, but he _____.
　　　　　　　　　　　　　　　　　our customers / popular / is / among

He came to Japan a month ago. _____ in
　　　　　　　　　　　　　a language school / he / is / at / a student
Shinjuku.

文法 一般動詞とbe動詞の復習

3 （　）の中に下の動詞を適切な形にして入れ、意味の通る文にしなさい。be動詞は2回以上用いられます。

I have a part-time job in Harajuku. My shift today begins at 5:00 p.m. I arrived at Shinjuku Station at 4:15 p.m. and (　) the 4:30 train. Just before Harajuku Station, the train (　) suddenly. Everyone on the train (　) quiet, and waited for the train to start. I called the store manager, but the phone (　) busy. I decided to (　) an email to Taku instead, but my cell phone battery (　) out.

be　　send　　take　　stop　　run

4 サトシはまたバイトを辞めました。絵と語句を参考にして下線部に当てはまる語句を記入しなさい。

例）A: Satoshi is looking for a job.
　　B: Really? He worked at <u>a convenience store</u>, didn't he?
　　A: Yes, but he quit his old job.
　　B: Why?
　　A: Because <u>his shift began late at night too often</u>.

① He worked at ＿＿＿＿＿＿, didn't he? / Because ＿＿＿＿＿＿.
② He worked at ＿＿＿＿＿＿, didn't he? / Because ＿＿＿＿＿＿.
③ He worked at ＿＿＿＿＿＿, didn't he? / Because ＿＿＿＿＿＿
　　＿＿＿＿＿＿.

イラストだけを見て会話してみましょう。

Lesson 6　アルバイト〔名詞を詳しく〕

■ Activities

（1）サトシはバイト先の居酒屋「桜横丁」で、インド人の新人にキッチンの仕事を説明しています。下の選択肢から適語を選んで（　）に入れ、Teriyaki Chickenの作り方の説明を完成させなさい。マニュアルカードとイラストを参考にしましょう。

　　It is easy to （　　　） the teriyaki chicken dish. Read Manual A-1.

① Take a pack of chicken （　　　） the freezer. It is on the second shelf from the bottom.
② （　　　） it in the microwave oven, and （　　　） it for 6 minutes.
③ Open the pack and put the chicken （　　　） the plate.
④ Take a pack of vegetables （　　　） the refrigerator. It is on the fourth shelf from the bottom.
⑤ （　　　） it in the microwave oven, and （　　　） it for 1 minute.
⑥ Open the pack and put the vegetables （　　　） the chicken. Serve.

　　　　　on　　by　　out of　　heat　　make　　put

Manual A-1
Teriyaki Chicken

〈Chicken〉
Freezer：Shelf 2
Microwave：6 min.

〈Vegetables〉
Refrigerator：Shelf 4
Microwave：1 min.

（2）マニュアルだけを見て言えるようにしましょう。

■ Let's Write

マニュアルカードとイラストを参照して、居酒屋「桜横丁」でのSpaghetti with Tomato Sauceの作り方を英語で書いてみましょう。

Manual B-3
Spaghetti with Tomato Sauce

〈Boiled Spaghetti〉
Refrigerator：Shelf 3
Microwave：4 min. 30 sec.

〈Tomato Sauce〉
Freezer：Shelf 3
Microwave：1 min.

Lesson 7

健康
〔Wh 疑問文①〕

■ Let's Try

下は病院内の様子です。この絵を2分間見て記憶してください。

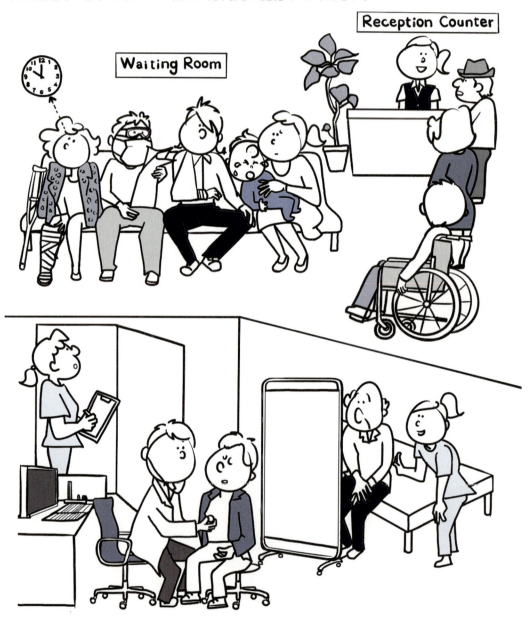

Lesson 7 健康〔Wh疑問文①〕

1 左の絵を見ないで、次の質問に対する正しい答えを選びましょう。

1. What is the man with glasses and a surgical mask reading?
   He is reading (a book / a newspaper / a magazine).

2. Where is the man in the wheelchair?
   He is (at the front of / in the middle of / at the end of) the line.

3. What is the woman in the coat looking at?
   She is looking at (the clock / her right leg / the nurse).

4. Who is sitting on the bed?
   (A little girl / An old man / A young boy) is sitting on the bed.

5. What time is it?
   It is (9:30 a.m. / 10:00 a.m. / 10:30 a.m.)

2 次の①〜④は左の絵の中の誰が言っているのでしょう。絵の中に番号を入れましょう。

① "Breathe in and out."
② "Take off your shoes and lie down on the bed."
③ "May I see your insurance card?"
④ "Mr. Koji Oda. Come in, please."

3 待合室のソファに座る４人の患者はこのあと診察を受けました。医師と話しているのはどの患者でしょう。

Doctor: What's the matter?
Patient: I have a runny nose, and I can't stop sneezing.
Doctor: Are your eyes itchy?
Patient: Yes, and they often get watery.
Doctor: Do you have a temperature?
Patient: No.
Doctor: You have hay fever.

<u>左から（　　）番目の患者</u>

Listening Check! T / F　１〜４の音声を聞いて、絵の内容に合っていればT、違っていればFを記入しましょう。

1. (　　　)　2. (　　　)　3. (　　　)　4. (　　　)

Words

病気・けが

1 右の症状にあてはまるものをイラスト内の①〜⑧から選んで、（　）に番号を入れましょう。

（　）headache
（　）bump on my forehead
（　）runny nose
（　）earache
（　）toothache
（　）sore shoulder
（　）pimple
（　）temperature

＊絵だけを見て I have a headache. のように言ってみましょう。

2 下の文にあてはまるものを①〜⑥のイラストから選んで、（　）に番号を入れましょう。

①  ②  ③

④  ⑤  ⑥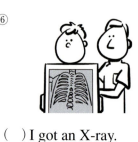

（　）I have hay fever.　（　）I have poor eyesight.　（　）I got an X-ray.
（　）I got a flu shot.　（　）I have an allergy to eggs.　（　）I broke my leg.

Let's Listen

3人の話を聞いて病名を選びなさい。

1. the flu / an allergy　**2.** poor eyesight / hay fever　**3.** a backache / a toothache

Lesson 7　健康〔Wh疑問文①〕

Exercises

文法 疑問詞を使った疑問文

1 次の文を英語で言うとき、どんな疑問詞を使いますか。

1. この画面にどうやってアクセスしたの？（　　　）　2. そのパーマ、どこでかけた？（　　　）
3. あしたは何を持っていけばいいんだっけ？（　　　）　4. そんなこと、誰が言ったの？（　　　）
5. これはどこに置いたらよろしいですか？（　　　）　6. 一体全体、何が起こったの？（　　　）
7. 次回はいつお越しいただけますか。（　　　）　8. お父様のお具合はいかがですか。（　　　）
9. どなたをお待ちですか？（　　　）

2 疑問詞を使った疑問文は〈疑問詞＋疑問文の形〉になります。例にならって、Q（疑問文）とWhQ（　　　部分を尋ねる疑問文）とに形を変えなさい。

例)　　　　　　　　　　He　　saw　　the doctor　　　last Friday .
　　Q　　　　　Did　　he　　see　　the doctor　　　last Friday ?
　　WhQ　When　did　　he　　see　　the doctor　　　　　　　　?

1.　　　　　　　　　　　The waiting room　　is　　on the first floor .
　　Q　_____　on the first floor ?
　　WhQ _____ ?

2.　　　　　　　　　　　The nurse　　put　　a Band-Aid　　on the cut.
　　Q　_____　a Band-Aid　_____ ?
　　WhQ _____ ?

3 尋ねる部分が主語の場合は〈疑問詞＋疑問文の形〉ではなく、〈疑問詞＋動詞の形〉になります。例にならって、WhQ（　　　部分を尋ねる疑問文）に形を変えなさい。

例)　　　　The medicine　　is　　in this bottle.
　　WhQ　　what　　　　　is　　in this bottle　　?

1.　　　　Taro　　　　　is　　behind the door.
　　WhQ　_____ ?

2.　　　　Mr. Saito　　has　　the flu.
　　WhQ　_____ ?

4 ＿＿＿の部分が答になるように（　）に適語を入れて会話を完成させましょう。

1. A:（　　　）（　　　）you（　　　）this medicine?
   B: I got it at BB Drug Store .

2. A:（　　　）（　　　）your next appointment with the doctor?
   B: It is the day after tomorrow .

3. A:（　　　）is your temperature?
   B: My temperature is 38.7 degrees Celsius .

5 （　）内の語を並べ替えて質問の文を完成させましょう。ただし、不要な語が1つ含まれています。

1. A:＿＿＿＿＿＿＿＿＿＿＿＿＿＿＿＿＿＿＿＿＿＿
   （the accident / when / was / did / happen）?
   B: It happened last evening around 6:00.

2. A:＿＿＿＿＿＿＿＿＿＿＿＿＿＿＿＿＿＿＿＿＿＿
   （absent / who / why / is / today）?
   B: Hiroshi is absent.

6 答に合った疑問文を自由に作りなさい。

1. A:＿＿＿＿＿＿＿＿＿＿＿＿＿＿＿＿＿＿＿＿＿＿＿＿？
   B: Last week.

2. A:＿＿＿＿＿＿＿＿＿＿＿＿＿＿＿＿＿＿＿＿＿＿＿＿？
   B: At the station.

3. A:＿＿＿＿＿＿＿＿＿＿＿＿＿＿＿＿＿＿＿＿＿＿＿＿？
   B: Yes, I was.

7 （　）の語を使って英文を作りなさい。

1. A「薬はどこでもらうのですか？」（the medicine）

   ＿＿＿＿＿＿＿＿＿＿＿＿＿＿＿＿＿＿＿＿＿＿＿＿
   B「お近くの調剤薬局です」（the local pharmacy）

   ＿＿＿＿＿＿＿＿＿＿＿＿＿＿＿＿＿＿＿＿＿＿＿＿

2. ファッションモデルはどうやって体重を減らすのですか？（lose weight）

   ＿＿＿＿＿＿＿＿＿＿＿＿＿＿＿＿＿＿＿＿＿＿＿＿

3. A「だれが救急車を呼んだのですか？」（the ambulance）

   ＿＿＿＿＿＿＿＿＿＿＿＿＿＿＿＿＿＿＿＿＿＿＿＿
   B「わたしです」

   ＿＿＿＿＿＿＿＿＿＿＿＿＿＿＿＿＿＿＿＿＿＿＿＿

Lesson 7 健康〔Wh疑問文①〕

■ Activities

健康調査表です。1～3の（　）に適語を入れて質問を完成させましょう。また、4にならって5と6の質問を作りなさい。好きなスポーツ、睡眠時間、食事のことなど、自由に作り、出来上がったらパートナーに質問して答えてもらいましょう。

Health Survey

1. (　　　) (　　　) (　　　) (　　　) for breakfast?
   I eat ☐rice ☐bread ☐cereal ☐others .

2. (　　　) (　　　) (　　　) (　　　) (　　　) (　　　) last?
   I saw the dentist ☐less than 1 month ago   ☐1- 6 months ago
   　　　　　　　　　☐7-12 months ago   ☐more than 1 year ago .

3. (　　　) (　　　) (　　　) (　　　) (　　　) ?
   ☐Yes, I take some supplements.   ☐No, I don't take any supplements.

4. What is your favorite food?
   _____

5. _____ ?
   _____

6. _____ ?
   _____

■ Let's Write

次のようなときに、あなたやあなたの家族はどんなことをしていますか？　あるいはしないようにしていますか？　書いてみましょう。

ストレスを感じたとき	ニキビができたとき
例) When I feel stressed, I eat a lot of pancakes.	例) When my brother has pimples, he stops eating chocolate.
体重を減らしたいとき	風邪をひいたとき

Lesson 8

ショッピング
〔Wh 疑問文②〕

🎧 Let's Try

サトシがオンラインショッピングをしています。下は商品情報と記入済みのオーダーフォームです。

This Week's Specials

Item No. 1 T-shirt ¥1,300	Item No. 2 Rain Boots ¥4,200	Item No. 3 Carry-on Luggage ¥11,500
size：S/M/L/XL color：black/white/purple/and more （click here for information） *Cotton 100% *Hand wash recommended	size：23.5/24.0/24.5 Type A：black and white stripe Type B：dotted Type C：flower print（Size 23.5 is out of stock.）	color：black/brown size：30 × 40.4 × 35.5 cm weight：3.5 kg *Four wheeled *Order soon. This item is very popular.
Item No. 4 Mineral Water ¥1,560	Item No. 5 Knit Cap ¥980	Item No. 6 Post-it Notes ¥900
12 bottles per pack （1 liter per bottle） *Not refundable	color：navy/cream/red/black size：M pattern：plain Polyester 80%, Wool 20% *Washable	6 pads per pack （100 sheets per pad） 152 mm × 102 mm *Only two left in stock. Order soon.

Order Form

Item No.	Size	Color	Quantity	Price	Sub total
1	XL	white	3	¥1,300	¥3,900
5	—	cream	1	¥980	¥980
Shipping					¥530
Total					¥5,410
Payment method	☑cash on delivery ☐credit card ☐ATM ☐convenience store				

Lesson 8　ショッピング〔Wh疑問文②〕

1　次の質問に日本語で答えましょう。
1. 返品ができない商品はどれですか？
2. ポストイットノート1冊の値段はいくらでしょうか？
3. ニット帽の素材は何ですか？
4. ミネラルウォーターを24リットル必要な場合、左の商品を何パック買えばよいでしょうか？
5. 雨用の長靴にはどんな柄がありますか？

2　次の質問に1は記号で、2〜4は英語で答えなさい。
1. Which of the following items is not in stock?　(　　)
   (a) A black carry-on luggage.
   (b) A pair of 23.5 cm flower print rain boots.
   (c) A pack of Post-it Notes.

2. How heavy is the carry-on luggage?　(　　　　　　　　　　　　)

3. How much is the shipping fee?　　　(　　　　　　　　　　　　)

4. How will he pay for his order?　　　(　　　　　　　　　　　　)

3　商品が配達されてからサトシは店に電話をしました。以下はそのときの会話の一部です。下から適語を選んで(　)に入れ、会話を完成させましょう。

Satoshi: I ordered a (　　　　) knit cap, but you sent me a red one. I want to make an (　　　　　　).
　Shop: I'm so sorry. May I (　　　　　　) your order number, sir?
Satoshi: 5389.
　Shop: What is (　　　　　　　　　　　)?
Satoshi: The item number is 5.
　Shop: We'll exchange the red cap (　　　　　　) a cream cap.

> the item number / for / cream / exchange / have

Listening Check!　**T / F**　1〜4の音声を聞いて、商品情報やオーダーフォームの内容に合っていればT、違っていればFを記入しましょう。

1. (　　　)　2. (　　　)　3. (　　　)　4. (　　　)

Words

商店と品物

次の商品はどの商品棚にあるでしょうか？　上の図の①〜⑭から選んで番号を記入しましょう。

( ) cabbage　　( ) yogurt　　( ) oolong tea　　( ) pork　　( ) coke

( ) glue　　( ) mayonnaise　　( ) canned tuna　　( ) salt　　( ) green pepper

( ) vinegar　　( ) cucumber　　( ) stapler　　( ) celery　　( ) tooth paste

( ) men's underwear　　( ) scissors　　( ) rice balls　　( ) watermelon　　( ) rice crackers

Let's Listen

1〜4の会話の話者たちはどの店にいる可能性が高いでしょうか？　①〜⑦から選びましょう。

1. (　)　　2. (　)　　3. (　)　　4. (　)

①Grocery store　②Electric appliance store　③Stationery shop
④CD rental shop　⑤Shoe store　⑥Dry-cleaner's　⑦Furniture store

Lesson 8　ショッピング〔Wh疑問文②〕

Exercises

《疑問詞＋形容詞 / 名詞》

1 次の日本語に合う疑問の表現は何でしょう？

〈数〉　　　①何枚のTシャツ　　（　　）（　　　　）T-shirts
〈量〉　　　②どれくらいの水　　（　　）（　　　　）water
〈程度〉　　③どれくらいの高さ　（　　　　）tall
〈どの〜〉　④どっちのお店　　　（　　　　）shop
〈何の〜〉　⑤何色　　　　　　　（　　　　）color
　　　　　　⑥何サイズ　　　　　（　　　　）size
〈だれの〜〉⑦だれのメガネ　　　（　　　　）glasses

2 次の日本語の意味を表すように、（　）に適語を書き入れましょう。
1. ピザを何切れ食べましたか？　（　　）（　　　）pieces of pizza did you eat?
2. 1日にどれくらいの水分をとりますか？
　　　　　　　　　　　　　　　（　　）（　　　）water do you drink a day?
3. どんな種類のパソコンを買ったのですか？
　　　　　　　　　　　　（　　）（　　　）（　　　）computer did you buy?
4. どちらの方向へ行けばよいのでしょうか？　（　　）（　　　）should I go?
5. どっちのお店がお薦めですか？　（　　　）（　　　）do you recommend?
6. 駅はどれくらい遠いのでしょう？　（　　　）（　　　）is the station?
7. この映画はどれくらい長いの？　（　　　）（　　　）is this movie?

3 空欄に適語を入れて、Q（疑問文）とWhQ（　　　部分を尋ねる疑問文）とに形を変えなさい。

1.　　　　　　　　　Tokyo Skytree　　is　　634 meters tall .
　Q　_____ 634 meters tall ?
　WhQ _____ _____ _____ ?

2.　　　　　　　　　　　You　went　abroad　three times .
　Q　　_____ _____ _____ _____ three times ?
　WhQ _____ _____ _____ _____ _____ ?

51

4 次の日本語に合うように、（　）の中の語を並び替えなさい。

1. 試験、どれくらい難しかったの？
(the exam / how / was / difficult)?
_____

2. 1日にコーヒーを何杯飲みますか？
(many / coffee / how / do / cups / you / of) drink every day ?
_____ drink every day ?

3. その財布、いくらだったの？
(that wallet / much / how / was)?
_____

4. その店はどんな服を売っているの？
(sell / what / they / do / clothes / of / kind) at the store?
_____ at the store?

文法《数量》

5 次のものはどのような語句で個数を表現するでしょうか？
例) a cup of tea, two cups of tea（× two teas）, many cups of tea

1. a carton of _____   2. a liter of _____
3. a bag of _____   4. a bottle of _____
5. a can of _____   6. a sheet of _____
7. a glass of _____   8. a tube of _____
9. a kilo of _____

Lesson 8　ショッピング〔Wh疑問文②〕

■ Activities　Student

Student B ▶ p. 90

B's shopping list

olive oil	(	) bottles
beer	(	) cans
cucumbers	(	)
tissue	(	) boxes
slippers	(	) pairs
T-shirts	(	)

（1）あなたはBさんから買い物を頼まれましたが、数が分かりません。Bさんに質問してリストを完成させてください。
　How many bottles of olive oil do you need? で会話を始めましょう。

（2）今度は、あなたがBさんに右の商品の買い物を頼みましたが、個数を伝え忘れました。Bさんからの質問に対して、I need …… などの表現を使って品物の個数を答えてください。

■ Let's Write

あなたはオンラインショップで白黒縞模様のレインブーツ24センチを購入しましたが、履いてみたら大きすぎるので23.5センチに交換しようと思います。オンラインショップにメールを書きましょう。注文番号は9462です。

Dear Customer Service:
_____
_____
_____
_____

Thank you in advance for your help. I look forward to hearing from you soon.

Best,
_____

Lesson 9

休日
〔時の表現〕

Let's Try

サトシはバイト先の留学生を東京バスツアーに誘おうと考えています。下はそのバスツアーのサイトです。

Four Hour Tokyo Bus Tour

Reservation

You will see the main sightseeing spots of Tokyo: Asakusa, the Sumida River (drive through), Tokyo Skytree and Akihabara (drive through).

- Tour schedule: Tuesdays, Thursdays, Saturdays beginning September 1 thru November 30.
  (Exceptions* are the fourth Tuesday, fourth Thursday and the day after national holidays. On these days, the bus tour will not be operating.)
- Departing times: Every two hours, on the hour. 9:00 a.m. – 5:00 p.m.
- Fare: Adults 3,000 yen / Children 1,800 yen
- Pick-up point: Ueno Bus Terminal
- Drop-off point: Ueno Bus Terminal

Asakusa

Tokyo Skytree

★★★★★★★ FAQ ★★★★★★★

Q1. How do I make a reservation?
　A1. You can make a reservation from this site. Click **Reservation** on the top of this page.
Q2. When do I pay for the tour?
　A2. You can pay on the day of the tour.
Q3. Are all the buses two-story buses?
　A3. Yes. All the buses are two-story buses with wide windows.

* exceptions 例外

Lesson 9　休日〔時の表現〕

1　サイトの内容に合っていればT、違っていればFを記入しましょう。
1. (　　) このツアーは東京の4つの名所すべてで下車する。
2. (　　) バスの出発時刻は午前9時、11時、午後1時、3時、5時である。
3. (　　) このツアーは1年を通して実施される。
4. (　　) 予約はこのページの Reservation で行う。
5. (　　) もしサトシが留学生2人と一緒に参加するならば合計金額は9000円になり、予約後1週間以内に振り込まなければならない。
6. (　　) すべてバスは2階建てである。

2　10月の予約状況は、3日、8日、26日が満席になっています。サイトの説明文と合わせて考え、 Reservation のページのカレンダーに記号（予約可○　満席×　運休△）を書き入れましょう。

October

Sun	Mon	Tue	Wed	Thu	Fri	Sat
		1	2	3	4	5
6	7	8	9	10	11	12
13	14	15	16	17	18	19
20	21	22	23	24	25	26
27	28	29	30	31		

3　正しい答えを選びましょう。
1. How many hours does this tour take?
   ── It takes (three hours / four hours).

2. If Satoshi takes the 11 o'clock bus tour, what time does he return to the Ueno Bus Terminal?
   ── He returns at (3:00 p.m. / 4:00 p.m.)

Listening Check!　T / F　1〜4の音声を聞いて、サイトの内容に合っていればT、違っていればFを記入しましょう。

1. (　　　)　2. (　　　)　3. (　　　)　4. (　　　)

Words

時を表す表現

1 会話中の下線部に、　　　から語を選んで書き入れましょう。繰り返して用いる語があります。

for　until　in　on　at　by　times　ago

① What time did you go to bed?
____ 4:00 a.m. ____ the morning.

② When were you born?
I was born ____ February 29th, 1910.

③ How long will you stay in Japan?
I'll stay here ____ 10 days.

④ How often do you practice judo?
Three ____ a week.

⑤ When is the deadline?
You have to finish it ____ tomorrow.

⑥ When does the store close?
It is open ____ 11:00 p.m.

⑦ Where are you going?
I will be back ____ a minute.

⑧ When did you get your driver's license?
I got it 3 days ____.

2 英語で書きなさい。また、読み方も書いてみましょう。

例）8月3日	August 3	August third
1. 3月31日		
2. 12月13日 (土)		
3. 2015年2月25日		
4. あなたの生年月日		

Let's Listen

1〜6の会話を聞いて、それぞれの会話に当てはまるイラストを選びなさい。また日付も数字で書き取りましょう。

1. (　) _____
2. (　) _____
3. (　) _____
4. (　) _____
5. (　) _____
6. (　) _____

a　b　c　d　e　f

Exercises

文法 時の表現

1 「時」の表現をまとめて示します。下線部に適切な前置詞を下から選んで書き入れ、（　）にはそれらの意味を番号で書き入れましょう。

◆ 日本語の「〜に」に相当するもの

1. (　) _____ 6:20 a.m.　_____ 7:00 o'clock　_____ noon
2. (　) _____ Monday　_____ July 20
3. (　) _____ January　_____ the spring　_____ 2015
4. (　) _____ the morning/afternoon/evening

◆ その他の表現

5. (　) I waited for the bus _____ two hours.
6. (　) I have to arrive at school _____ 8:55 a.m.
7. (　) Stay here _____ 1:00 o'clock.
8. (　) The bus leaves _____ ten minutes.
9. (　) _____ this/next/last/every week

〈前置詞〉	on ／ at ／ until ／ in ／ for ／ by ／ ×（前置詞不要）
〈意味〉	①月、季節、年　②〜の間（期間）　③午前、午後、夜　④時刻　⑤〜後に（あと〜で）　⑥〜までには　⑦曜日、日　⑧この/次の/この前の/毎〜　⑨〜までずっと

2 下線部に at ／ on ／ in ／ ×（前置詞不要）のいずれかを書きなさい。

1. _____ July
2. _____ July 19th
3. _____ 2019
4. _____ 11:00 p.m.
5. _____ next month
6. _____ noon
7. _____ every Wednesday
8. _____ Monday

3 適切な語を入れなさい。

1. 明日までずっと　　（　　　　）tomorrow
2. 4日前に　　　　　four days（　　　　）
3. 2週間の間　　　　（　　　　）two weeks
4. 8時までには　　　（　　　　）eight o'clock
5. あと3時間で　　　（　　　　）three hours
6. 年に5回　　　　　five（　　　　）a year
7. あさって　　　　　the day（　　　　）tomorrow
8. おととい　　　　　the day（　　　　）yesterday

4 下のカレンダーにはサトシの６月の予定が書かれています。今日が６月18日と仮定し、下の文章中の（　）に①〜⑥の語句から適切なものをあてはめ、文章を完成させましょう。

June

Sun	Mon	Tue	Wed	Thu	Fri	Sat
	1 バイト/ジム	2 部活	3 バイト	4 部活	5 部活	6
7	8 バイト	9 部活	10 バイト/ジム	11 部活	12 部活	13
14 実家	15 バイト/ジム	誕生日 16 部活	17 バイト	18 部活	19 部活	20 県大会
21	22 バイト	23 部活	24 バイト/ジム	25 部活	26 部活	27
28 実家	29 バイト/ジム	30 部活				

　Satoshi has judo practice（　　）. His teammates celebrated his birthday（　　）. He works part-time（　　）. The Prefectural Judo Tournament is（　　）. He goes to the gym（　　）. He goes home to Nagano（　　）to see his girlfriend.

① three times a week　② once a week　③ the day before yesterday
④ twice a week　⑤ every two weeks　⑥ the day after tomorrow

5 図の①から⑦について、それぞれ時間と行動を表す文を作りなさい。

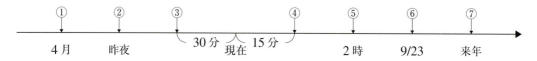

①４月　②昨夜　③30分　現在　15分　⑤２時　⑥9/23　⑦来年

	主語	動作	
①	school	begin	例) School began in April.
②	Mom	call me	
③	I	leave home	
④	the bus	come	例) The bus will come in 15 minutes.
⑤	I	meet Yuki	
⑥	I	make a reservation for the bus tour	
⑦	I	get a driver's license	

Lesson 9　休日〔時の表現〕

■ Activities　Student A　　　　　　　　　　Student B ▶ p. 91

あなたはBさんと来週中に1回一緒に出かけたいと思っています。下の自分のスケジュールを見ながら相手と都合を尋ね合って、2人とも都合の良い日時の候補を3つあげなさい。

例）　質問：How about Tuesday afternoon?
　　　答　：I'm sorry, it's impossible. I have to ・・・・. / OK, it's possible.

Student A

August	afternoon	evening
3 Sun		Driving school 5:00 p.m.
4 Mon		
5 Tue		Part-time job at JJ Super Market
6 Wed	Volunteer work　until 8:30 p.m. →	
7 Thu	Dentist	
8 Fri		
9 Sat	Go shopping with K	

■ Let's Write

上のActivitiesで日時の候補があがったら、次にどこに行くかを決めます。2人で相談して、下の4つのプランのうち可能なものの中から1つ選び、「いつ」「どこに」行って、「何を」する予定かを書きましょう。

Sunset Dinner Cruise Every day except Thursday 6:30 p.m. & 8:00 p.m. 　（90-minute cruise） Dinner: French Course ¥10,000 　　　　Italian Course ¥8,000	Aquarium Open：10:00 a.m. – 5:00 p.m. 　（Restaurant 11:30 a.m.~） 　（Coffee shop 10:00 a.m.~） Closed：Mondays & first Friday of the month Dolphin show：10:30 a.m., 1:00 p.m. & 3:30 p.m.
Fireworks Festival August 4th & 7th Fireworks：7:30 – 8:30 p.m. Yukata Contest：8:30 p.m. Food stands: hotdogs, fried noodles, roasted corn, shaved ice, etc.	Saturday Night Jazz Concert Saturdays, 6:00 – 8:00 p.m. ¥5,000（A glass of wine is included） You can dance to music from 7:30 to 8:00 p.m.

　　　　We will _____
　　　　_____
　　　　_____
　　　　_____

Lesson 10

大学生活
〔助動詞〕

Let's Try

大学祭で柔道部はヤキソバの模擬店を出すことになり、部長のサトシは当日の仕事分担を決めなければなりません。下はサトシが4人の部員に出したメールと、それに対する返事です。

From Satoshi
Sub YAKISOBA booth

We have only two weeks left before the festival. I am making the time schedule for the day. Can you help all day? If not, let me know when you will be unavailable* ASAP*.
Let's raise a lot of money and hold our summer training camp in Hokkaido!

*unavailable 都合が悪い *ASAP : as soon as possible

From Ayana
Sub Re: YAKISOBA booth

I'm scheduled to sing a gospel song on stage from 10:00 a.m. to 10:30 a.m. Before that, I have a rehearsal. It'll take at least two hours.
Come and see me on stage if you can.

From Kumi
Sub Re: YAKISOBA booth

I have to drive my grandmother to the hospital in the afternoon, so I have to leave school about 12:30 p.m.

From Kantaro
Sub Re: YAKISOBA booth

From 8:00 a.m. to 9:30 a.m., I will be standing in front of the main entrance to welcome guests as a member of the Festival Executive Committee.* I will be wearing a penguin costume!! So embarrassing*!

From Taku
Sub Re: YAKISOBA booth

I have to go to the Driver Licensing Center to take a driver's test, so I have to leave school about 10:30 a.m. Sorry, I can't come back to school later that day.

---

* a member of the Festival Executive Committee 大学祭実行委員　* embarrassing はずかしい

Lesson 10　大学生活〔助動詞〕

1　メールの内容に合っていればT、違っていればFを記入しましょう。

1. (　　) 大学祭まであと1週間である。
2. (　　) この企画で得た利益は合宿の資金に当てられる。
3. (　　) 当日9:00頃、ゴスペルのリハーサルが行われているはずである。
4. (　　) カンタローはペンギンの着ぐるみを着てヤキソバのPRに努める覚悟である。
5. (　　) タクは当日、運転免許試験を受けに行く予定である。

2　4人の返信メールを読んで、他に予定が入っていて都合がつかない時間帯を下の表に⟵⟶で記入しましょう。

	8	9	10	11	12	13	14	15
Ayana								
Kumi								
Kantaro								
Taku								

3　サトシはどんな仕事の分担表を作成したのでしょうか。　　　に担当者名を入れましょう。

Time Schedule		
8:00 〜 9:30	Set up a tent 1 person : ＿＿＿	Buy and bring ingredients (by car) 1 person : ＿＿＿
10:00 〜 12:00	Cook and sell yakisoba 2 persons : ＿＿＿　＿＿＿	
12:00 〜 15:00	2 persons : ＿＿＿　＿＿＿	

Listening Check! T / F　1〜4の音声を聞いて、メールの内容に合っていればT、違っていればFを記入しましょう。

1. (　　　)　2. (　　　)　3. (　　　)　4. (　　　)

学年暦

大学生活の1年間の行事を表しています。①〜⑥と⑦〜⑫に対応する語句を下の選択肢から選び、記号で書き入れましょう。

Spring Semester
Spring
①入学式　②履修登録　③奨学金申込　④期末試験
Summer
⑤外部実習　⑥海外研修

(　)　(　)　(　)　(　)　(　)　(　)

Fall Semester
Fall
⑦防災訓練　⑧大学祭　⑨就職説明会　⑩期末試験
Winter
⑪卒業式　⑫ゼミ合宿

(　)　(　)　(　)　(　)　(　)　(　)

Spring Semester	Fall Semester
a. study abroad	**g.** university festival
b. final exams	**h.** job guidance
c. scholarship application	**i.** final exams
d. course registration	**j.** seminar camp
e. internship	**k.** emergency drill
f. entrance ceremony	**l.** graduation ceremony

Let's Listen

就職相談室でヨースケが面談を受けています。面談の会話を聞いて、メモ書きの　　　の中の当てはまるものを選んで○で囲みましょう。

Name: Yosuke Imai　**Age:** 20 / 21　**Major:** Sociology / Economics
Skills: cash register / business software / bookkeeping
Work Experience (part-time job): pizza delivery / cashier
Other information: valid driver's license / tennis circle / drama club

Exercises

文法 助動詞・be going to・have to

助動詞（can / will / should / ...）や be going to / have to は原形動詞の前に来て、動詞の意味に話し手の気持ちを加えます。

（1）助動詞 can（〜できる） will（〜するだろう） should（〜すべき）などの語順

肯定文		We	can	make	the deadline.
否定文		We	can't	make	the deadline.
疑問文	Can	we		make	the deadline?

（2）be going to（〜することになっている）は be 動詞の語順になり、have to（〜しなければならない） don't have to（〜しなくてもいい）は一般動詞の語順になります。

---

1 指示に従って書き換えなさい。

1. We will have a rehearsal <u>at our university cafeteria</u>.（下線部を尋ねる文に）

2. You are going to wear a suit and tie to the Graduation Ceremony.（疑問文に）

3. We have to go to the training camp.（「しなくてもいい」に）

4. He had to pay <u>¥20,000</u>.（下線部を尋ねる文に）

2 can か should を使って、それぞれの目的にかなった英文を書きなさい。

1. あと 10 分待ってほしいと頼みましょう。（ for another ten minutes ）

2. 前のガールフレンドには会うべきではないと忠告しましょう。（ ex-girlfriend ）

3. 授業を早退してよいか尋ねましょう。（ leave class early ）

4. ぜひ柔道部に入部すべきだと勧誘しましょう。（ join ）

3 （　）の中に、shouldn't / couldn't / have toのいずれかを補って会話を完成させ、パートナーと練習しましょう。

Yuki： Hi, Kumi! You don't look happy. Is something wrong?
Kumi： I was going to <u>finish course registration</u> yesterday, but I (　　　　　).
Yuki： You don't (　　　　　) worry, Kumi. The deadline is tomorrow.
Kumi： Really? Thank you, Yuki!

次に下線部を下の表現と入れ替えて、パートナーと練習しましょう。
(a) finish my Economics class report
(b) apply for next year's internship

4 Aさんの「どうして～しなかったの？」という質問に対してBさんは「～できなかったから」あるいは「～しければならなかったから」と言い訳します。couldn't / had toのいずれかと（　）内の語を用い、例にならってAさんの質問とBさんの言い訳を作りなさい。

例）A（do your homework） B（find）
①A（study abroad） B（enough money, save）
②A（yesterday, practice judo） B（the library, do research）
③A（take a trip to Taiwan） B（a mid-term exam, take）
④A（last night, give me a call） B（your phone number, remember）
⑤A（last Friday, come to class） B（go to a job interview）

例）A： <u>Why didn't you do your homework?</u>　　B： <u>I couldn't find my textbook.</u>
① A： _____　　B： _____
② A： _____　　B： _____
③ A： _____　　B： _____
④ A： _____　　B： _____
⑤ A： _____　　B： _____

Lesson 10　大学生活〔助動詞〕

■ Activities　Student A

Student B ▶ p. 92

(1) 今学期に「心理学Ⅰ」を履修しようと考えているあなたは、Bさんにアドバイスを求めることにしました。次の表現を参考にして、「心理学Ⅰ」の単位を取るために必要なことをBさんに質問してメモをとりましょう。

　　あなた：Do I have to write many reports?
　　Bさん：Yes, you have to ＿＿＿. / No, you don't have to ＿＿＿.
　　あなた：Thank you for your advice. Probably I will　または shouldn't take the course.

Psychology Ⅰ〔メモ〕
・write many reports
・read a lot of books
・make a presentation
・take an exam
---

(2) 今度は役割を交代して、あなたがBさんにアドバイスする番です。Bさんは「政治学Ⅱ」の授業について質問してきます。

Politics Ⅱ	
You have to:	**You don't have to:**
・do research before every class	・write a report
・take a final exam	・make a presentation

■ Let's Write

あなたがこれまでに履修した科目や、現在履修中の科目の中から、後輩に薦めたい授業を1つ選び、Activitiesで使われた語句や表現を参考にして、英語で科目説明の文章を書きましょう。

Lesson 11

世界の国々
〔比較級と最上級〕

Let's Try

1 地図中の①〜⑥の国名とその国にある都市名を下から選び、書き入れましょう。

国名	都市	国名	都市
①		④	
②		⑤	
③		⑥	

国　名：Egypt　　South Africa　　Turkey　　Korea　　China　　Peru
都市名：Beijing　　Seoul　　　　　Lima　　　Cairo　　Istanbul　Cape Town

Lesson 11 世界の国々〔比較級と最上級〕

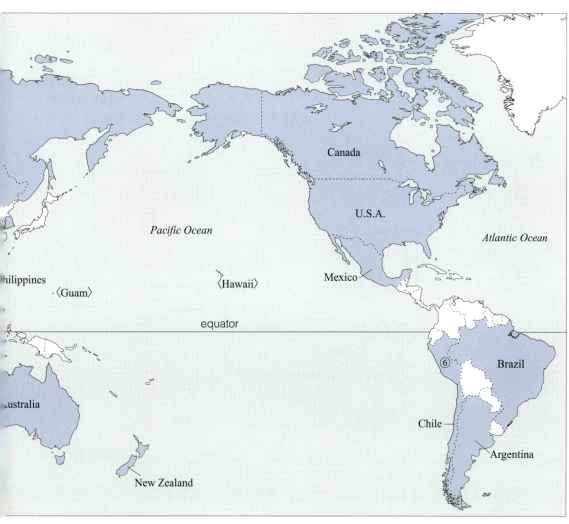

2 次の文は地図中のどの国を説明しているでしょうか？ 国名を書きましょう。

1. This country is famous for koalas and kangaroos. (　　　　)
2. Alaska is one of the states in this country. (　　　　)
3. This is the largest country in South America. (　　　　)
4. People in this country eat hot and spicy food, and curry is from this country. (　　　　)
5. Madrid is the capital city of this country. (　　　　)
6. In this country, the average winter temperature is below zero degrees Celsius. It is next to Sweden. (　　　　)

Listening Check! T / F　1〜4の音声を聞いて、内容が正しければT、間違っていればFを記入しましょう。

1. (　　　) 　2. (　　　) 　3. (　　　) 　4. (　　　)

Words

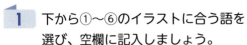

天　気

1 下から①～⑥のイラストに合う語を選び、空欄に記入しましょう。

① [　　　　] ② [　　　　]
③ [　　　　] ④ [　　　　]
⑤ [　　　　] ⑥ [　　　　]

sunny　windy　cloudy
rainy　humid　snowy

2 　　から適切な語を選んで温度計の㋐～㋒に書き入れ、会話文を練習しましょう。

warm　　hot
cold　　cool
freezing

〈会話〉
A: What is the temperature today?
B: It's twenty degrees Celsius. It is warm today.

(　　) ㋐
(warm) ㋑
(　　) ㋒
(　　) ㋓
(　　) ㋔

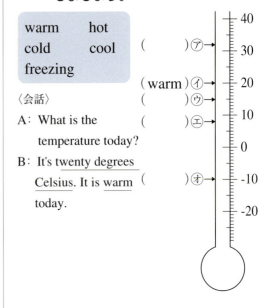

世界の国々

①～⑭に当てはまるものを、a)～n)から選び、表を完成させましょう。

国名	言語	首都	国名	言語	首都	
Japan	①	Tokyo	⑦	⑧	Berlin	a) Arabic
China	②	Beijing	France	⑨	⑩	b) Chinese
Spain	③	④	Brazil	⑪	⑫	c) Germany
Egypt	⑤	⑥	India	⑬	⑭	d) Madrid

e) Portuguese　f) Brasilia　g) French　h) Hindi　i) New Delhi
j) Spanish　k) Cairo　l) German　m) Japanese　n) Paris

Let's Listen

天気予報を聞いて、右の図中の(　)に気温(最高/最低)を数字で書き入れ、また□には下から当てはまるものを選び、記号で答えましょう。

A: ☀　　B: ☃
C: ☁⇒☀　D: ☂⇒☀

Sapporo (　) / -7 ☀
Sendai　5 / (　) □
Tokyo　(　) / 11 □
Osaka　10 / 4 ☁/☂
Fukuoka (　) / 3 □
Naha　18 / 13 ☂

Lesson 11　世界の国々〔比較級と最上級〕

Exercises

文法　比較級・最上級

「(…より) もっと〜」という比較級には形容詞・副詞に -er の語尾をつけるか、more を単語の前につけます。「一番〜」という最上級には形容詞・副詞に -est の語尾をつけるか、most を単語の前につけます。

1 例にならって文を完成させましょう。

例)	Mt. Everest is higher than Mt. Fuji.
(high / low)	It is the highest mountain in the world. Mt. Asama is the lowest of the three.
① Seoul: -5℃　Sendai: 4℃　Los Angeles: 18℃　(cold / warm)	Seoul _____ Sendai.　It _____ of the three.　Los Angeles _____ of the three.
② ¥130,000 成田から→NY　羽田から→那覇 ¥18,700　成田から→Hawaii ¥90,000　(expensive / cheap)	The ticket to NY _____ the ticket to Hawaii.　It _____.　The ticket to Okinawa _____.

2 下の表を参考にして、英文の (　　) に適語を補い、文章を完成させましょう。

面積の大きい国		
Rank	Country	Area (km²)
1	Russia	17,100,000
2	Canada	9,980,000
3	U.S.A.	9,630,000
4	China	9,600,000
……	……	……
61	Japan	380,000

　There are more than one hundred countries in the world. There are large or small countries. The U.S.A. is a large country, and it is (　　) (　　) China, but it is (　　) (　　) Canada and Russia. Actually, (　　) is the largest country in the world, and (　　) is the third largest.

3 例を参考に、**1**〜**4**の枠からそれぞれ単語を1つずつ取り上げて組み合わせ、文を作りましょう。組み合わせは1つとは限りません。

1 Paris, Sydney, Tokyo Skytree, Kyoto, soccer, the Vatican City	**2** large, beautiful, tall, popular, small	**3** city, building, sightseeing spot, country, sport	**4** Australia, Europe, Japan, the world

例) Paris is the most beautiful city in Europe.

1. _____
2. _____
3. _____

文法 《 want to do 》

4 どこの国に行って何をしたいかを話題にしている会話です。（　）内の語を使って文を完成させましょう。答を合わせたら下の絵を使って練習しましょう。

A: _____ visit?
　　(country / you / which / want / do / to)
B: I want to visit England.
A: _____ England?
　　(to / you / in / what / do / want / do)
B: I want to go to Big Ben.

例) ヒント go	ヒント the Great Wall / see	ヒント ride / a camel

5 日本語の意味を表すように（　）に適語を入れて文を完成させてから、その質問への答えを英語で書きましょう。

1. エジプトでは何語が話されているのですか？　（　　）（　　） do they （　　） in （　　）? — _____
2. カナダとアメリカではどちらが面積が広いですか？　（　　） is （　　）, Canada or the U.S.A? — _____
3. 今あなたがいる場所の天気はどうですか？　（　　）（　　） the weather （　　） your town now? — _____
4. どの国に旅行したいですか？　（　　）（　　）（　　） you （　　）（　　） visit? — _____

Lesson 11 世界の国々〔比較級と最上級〕

■ Activities　Student A　　　　　　　　Student B ▶ p. 93

(1) 例を参考にしてパートナーに勉強したい言語とその理由を尋ね、会話をしてみましょう。答えをよく聞き、下の表を埋めましょう。スペルが分らないときには英語で How do you spell ~? と言い、日本語は使わないこと！

　　あなた：Now I have a question. Which language do you plan to study next?
　パートナー：I plan to study Hindi.
　　あなた：Why do you want to study Hindi?
　パートナー：Because I want to eat real curry in India.

例)	パートナーの答	あなた自身の情報
言語　［Hindi］ 国名　（India） 目的　to eat real curry	［　　　　　］ （　　　　　） to _____	［　German　］ （　Germany　） to play soccer

(2) 今度は役割を交代してパートナーの質問に答えましょう。聞きとれないときには、Could you say that again ? と言い、日本語は使わないこと！

■ Let's Write

次の2つの旅行計画のうち1つを選ぶとしたら、あなたはどちらを選びますか？　2つの計画をいろいろな項目について比較し、選んだ理由を英文で書いてみましょう。

	Plan A	Plan B
Destination	Hawaii / U.S.A.	Vancouver / Canada
Length	4 days	a week
Flight from Narita（cost）	8 hours（¥90,000）	11 hours（¥89,000）
Hotel	¥10,000 per night Open since 1969 Convenient for shopping	¥5,500 per night Opened this spring
Activities	Surfing & Scuba diving	Snowboarding
AverageTemperature in Jan.	22.4℃	2.9℃

Lesson 12　海外旅行（1）

Let's Try

ヨーロッパ地図を眺めてみましょう。

Lesson 12 海外旅行 (1)

1 下の①〜⑧の都市は日本語で何と呼ばれていますか。また何という国にありますか。

都市名		国名	
(英語)	(日本語)	(英語)	(日本語)
① Rome			
② Athens			
③ Copenhagen			
④ Vienna			
⑤ Frankfurt			
⑥ Stockholm			
⑦ Amsterdam			
⑧ Zurich			

2 ケンタとサヤカ夫妻がヨーロッパ旅行の計画をたてています。2人の会話を聞いて（　）を埋めましょう。

S : I want to begin our journey from Germany. I'm interested in the (①　　　) of Germany.

K : All right. Let's use a direct (②　　　) to Frankfurt from Narita, and then take a train from Frankfurt to Berlin.

S : That sounds nice. Let's go (③　　　) in Berlin. I want to see the historical spots.

K : After that, I want to go to Austria. Let's go to Vienna by plane.

S : What do you want to do in Vienna?

K : Vienna is a city of classical (④　　　), so I want to attend a classical concert, opera or ballet performance. What country shall we visit after Austria?

S : How about (⑤　　　)? I want to try real pizza and pasta at a stylish restaurant. Can we visit two cities in Italy?

K : Yes, I think so. Where do you want to visit?

S : (⑥　　　) and Venice. I want to take a gondola ride in Venice.

K : All right. It will be better to go to Venice first, and then to Rome. Let's take a (⑦　　　) from Vienna to Venice. And, how about taking a (⑧　　　) from Venice to Rome? It takes less than (⑨　　　) hours from Venice to Rome.

S : Good idea! Where shall we go after Italy?

K : Of course.........Tokyo Narita.

S : Oh!

3 2人のヨーロッパでの旅行ルートはどのようになるのでしょう。飛行機移動は→、列車移動は⇢で、左ページの地図に記入しましょう。

Words

空の旅

 Departure

 Check-in Counter

 Security Check

 On the Plane

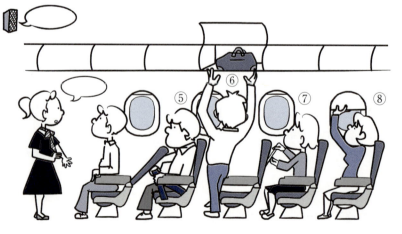

Lesson 12　海外旅行（1）

 Arrival

 Immigration / Passport Control　 Baggage Claim　 Currency Exchange

　 Customs　

1 下のA～Gのせりふはイラストのどの◯◯◯で言われていますか。◯◯◯にA～Gを入れましょう。

A. "Do you have anything in your pockets?"　B. "What's the purpose of your visit?"
C. "Return your seat to the upright position."　D. "Window seat or aisle seat?"
E. "Turn off all electronic devices."　F. "Sightseeing."
G. "I want to exchange Japanese yen into euro."

2 下のa～hの英語が表す動作をイラスト中の①～⑧から選び、（　）に書き入れましょう。

a. (　) put your bag in the overhead compartment　　b. (　) fasten your seatbelt
c. (　) take off your shoes　　d. (　) fold up the tray table
e. (　) take out all liquids and throw them away
f. (　) pull up the window shade　　g. (　) take everything out of your pockets
h. (　) take out the computer from your bag and put it on the tray

3 英語では何と言うのでしょう。▢の①～⑨から選びましょう。

(　)（空港で）荷物を預ける　　(　) 搭乗券　　(　) 機内持ち込み手荷物
(　) 手荷物預り証　　(　) 遅延　　(　) 帰りの航空券
(　) 出発　　(　) 到着　　(　) 目的地

①return ticket　②delay　③boarding pass　④claim tag　⑤destination
⑥carry-on baggage　⑦arrival　⑧departure　⑨check in

Let's Listen

ＣＤを聞いて＿＿部を埋め、パートナーと練習しましょう。次に下線部＿＿を□内の語に置き換えて練習してみましょう。

CD 56 1. チェックインカウンターで（A=航空会社の社員　B=旅行者）

　A：How many bags would you like to check in?
　B：Two. Can I ① ＿＿＿＿ this bag with me?
　A：No problem. This is your ② ＿＿＿＿ ③ ＿＿＿＿. Boarding begins at 11:20 a.m.
　B：What's the ④ ＿＿＿＿ ⑤ ＿＿＿＿?
　A：Gate 33. Please go to Gate 33 by 11:20 a.m.

　　| 9:15 a.m.　/　Gate 51 |

CD 57 2. 入国審査で（A=係官　B=旅行者）

　A：Next! .... Passport ....What's the ⑥ ＿＿＿＿ of your ⑦ ＿＿＿＿?
　B：Sightseeing.
　A：⑧ ＿＿＿＿ ⑨ ＿＿＿＿ will you stay?
　B：Five days.
　A：Do you have a ⑩ ＿＿＿＿ ⑪ ＿＿＿＿?
　B：Yes.
　A：Have a nice trip.

　　| To study　/　three weeks |

CD 58 3. 両替所で（A=旅行者　B=職員）

　A：Hello. I want to ⑫ ＿＿＿＿ Japanese ⑬ ＿＿＿＿ into US dollars.
　B：How much yen, sir?
　A：30,000 yen. And, can I have some ⑭ ＿＿＿＿ ⑮ ＿＿＿＿?
　B：Sure. Please ⑯ ＿＿＿＿ ⑰ ＿＿＿＿ this form, and hand me your ⑱ ＿＿＿＿.
　A：Here you are.
　B：Thank you.

　　| euro　/　40,000 yen |

76

Lesson 12　海外旅行(1)

4．観光案内所で（A=旅行者　B=職員）

A：I'm going to stay in this city for two days, and I want to ⑲_____
⑳_____. Can you recommend any places to visit?

B：Yes. ㉑_____ ㉒_____ ㉓_____ go to the old castle? It was built in the sixteenth century and has a lovely garden. If it's sunny, you can ㉔_____ a cup of tea there.

A：That sounds nice. How do I ㉕_____ ㉖_____?

B：You can take the No.3 bus from Central Station.

A：I see. Thank you very much.

> for one week　/　take the No.5 tram from East Station

Let's Write

これから海外旅行に出かけるあなたは、空港に着いてから飛び立つまでにすべきことを忘れないようメモしました。このメモに従ってあなたがとる行動を英文で書いてみましょう。

チェックインカウンター
　□スーツケース預け
　□搭乗券受け取り

セキュリティーチェック
　□PC出す
　□飲み物捨てる

搭乗　ゲート58　11：15までに

機内　□荷物片づけ
　　　□携帯切る
　　　□シートベルト

I go to the check-in counter.
I check in my suitcase.

Lesson 13

海外旅行（2）

■ Let's Try

サトシは念願のヨーロッパ旅行に出かけ、たくさんの思い出を作って帰ってきました。

①

		TICKET-RESERVATION					
					01	ADULT	
Date	Time	From	⇒ To	Date	Time	Class
8/29	08:37	COPENHAGEN	⇒ STOCKHOLM	8/29	13:50	2

TRAIN 530　COACH 6　SEAT NUMBER 37　PRICE：EURO ***9.00

②
ABC AIR

BOARDING PASS
ECONOMY CLASS

NAME OF PASSENGER　　　FLIGHT　　DATE
AMEMIYA/SATOSHI MR　　 AY667　　 AUG 31
FROM
COPENHAGEN　　CPH

GATE	BOARDING TIME	SEAT
35	17:10	19E

TO
ZURICH　　ZRH

TICKET INFORMATION
2　105　9548136831

③
★★★
HOTEL　HOLIDAY
ZURICH
Guest Name ： Mr. S. Amemiya
Room ： 261
Arrival Date ： Aug. 31
Departure Date ： Sept. 03

Guest Signature ：　*S. Amemiya*

④
VALID TODAY ONLY

Sun. Sep. 03

ADULT　　£11.00

WELCOME TO
THE TOWER OF LONDON

HER MAJESTY'S PALACE AND FORTRESS
THE TOWER OF LONDON

⑤
THE DOMINION THEATRE
TOTTENHAM COURT ROAD, LONDON
THE PHANTOM OF THE OPERA
MON. SEP. 4　　　　　7:45 PM
SEAT　　　　　　　　R43
TICKET PRICE：£35.00
SOLD FOR：£17.50 + £2.50 SERVICE CHARGE

the
HALF
PRICE
TICKET
BOOTH

Lesson 13　海外旅行(2)

1 前ページの①〜⑤は、サトシが使ったチケット類を使用した順に並べたものです。①〜⑤は次のどれでしょう。

　　(　　) 観光名所の入場券
　　(　　) 搭乗券
　　(　　) ミュージカルのチケット
　　(　　) 列車指定席券
　　(　　) ホテルのルームカード

2 前ページの①〜⑤について質問に答えなさい。

① (1)何時に列車はコペンハーゲンを出ましたか？
　　(2)コペンハーゲンからストックホルムまではどのくらいかかりますか？
　　(3)予約料金はいくらですか？

② (1)どこからこの便に乗りましたか？
　　(2)行き先はどこですか？
　　(3)この日午後5時に、サトシは機内にいましたか？

③ (1)このホテルはどこにありますか？
　　(2)何泊しましたか？
　　(3)いつチェックアウトしましたか？

④ (1)料金はいくらですか？
　　(2)ここを訪れたのはいつですか？
　　(3)このチケットは翌日も使用可能ですか？

⑤ (1)上演されたミュージカルのタイトルは何ですか？
　　(2)サトシは半額チケット売り場で、いくらでこのチケットを手に入れましたか？
　　(3)正規のチケット価格はいくらですか？

3 下はサトシの旅程表です。

1. この課の1ページ目と2ページ目をヒントにして、　　　を埋めて表を完成させましょう。

Travel/Activity Itinerary	
Aug. 27	Depart Narita for Copenhagen by plane.
28	Sightseeing old castles and the Little Mermaid Statue.
29	Travel to (1)　　　　　 by (2)　　　　　.
30	Shopping and dining at a local restaurant.
31	Back to Copenhagen by train. Leave for Zurich by (3)　　　　　.
Sept. 1	Visit Jungfraujoch* and the Alps.
2	A ferry trip on the lake.
3	Travel to London by plane. Visit (4)　　　　　 by bus.
4	See a (5)　　　　　.
5	Depart London and return to Narita by plane.

*Jungfraujoch：ユングフラウヨッホ（山の名前）

2. 正しい答えを選びましょう。

(1) Did he see the Little Mermaid Statue in Copenhagen?
(Yes, he did. / No, he didn't.)

(2) Where did he stay on August 30?
He stayed (in Copenhagen / in Stockholm).

(3) Where did he take a ferry?
He took a ferry (in Switzerland / in Sweden).

(4) Where was he on September 4?
He was (in Zurich / in London).

(5) How many times did he travel by plane during the trip?
He traveled by plane (three times / four times).

Lesson 13 海外旅行（2）

4 帰ってきてからサトシはブログに次のように書いています。（　）内の正しいほうを選びましょう。

I visited four countries — (① Denmark / Germany), (② Norway / Sweden), Switzerland and the UK. At the Immigration Counter of Copenhagen Airport, the officer said to me, "Welcome to (③ Europe / England)." Yes, at last I was in the EU!

I traveled between Copenhagen and Stockholm by (④ plane / train). The temperature was sometimes under 15℃ in Stockholm. I went (⑤ fishing / shopping) in a down jacket.

After returning to Copenhagen, I flew to Zurich (⑥ the next day / on the same day). Switzerland is famous for (⑦ its Alps / the Himalayas). The mountain railway took me up to the (⑧ highest / busiest) railway station in Europe. This station is 3,454 meters above sea level. It was a wonderland of snow and ice.

And then London! I stayed in London for (⑨ two / three) nights. On the first day, I took a red double-decker (⑩ ferry / bus) and visited the Tower of London. The next day I went to the Half Price Ticket Booth to get a ticket for (⑪ a musical / an opera). I wanted to see *The Notre Dame de Paris* but all the tickets were (⑫ sold out / take out), so I got a ticket for *The Phantom of the Opera* instead. The show was so exciting! I had a (⑬ terrific / terrible) time on the last night of my trip.

5 コペンハーゲンからロンドンまで、サトシはどのように移動したのでしょうか。飛行機は→、列車は⇢で、Lesson 12のヨーロッパ地図（p. 72）に書き込みましょう。

 **Let's Write**

2週間の海外旅行に行けるとしたら、いつ、どんなところに、どのように行って、どんなことをしたいですか？　旅程表を作成してから、英文にしてみましょう。旅程表は日本語でもかまいません。

Travel / Activity Itinerary				
Date	City	Country	Transportation	Things to do and see

Lesson 13　海外旅行(2)

Activities Student B

Student A ▶ p. 11

（1）下のFamily TreeはAさんのものです。下の質問例を参考にして、右の6人の年齢は何歳なのか、パートナーとはどんな関係なのかを質問し、AさんのFamily Treeを完成させましょう。

質問例 年齢を尋ねる場合…How old is Taiko?
関係を尋ねる場合…Is she your cousin?（Who is she? と尋ねてはいけません。）

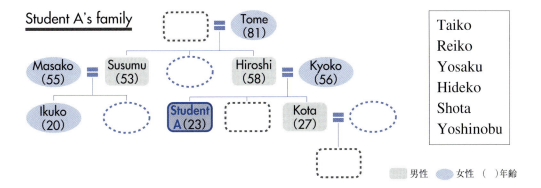

Taiko
Reiko
Yosaku
Hideko
Shota
Yoshinobu

■男性　●女性　（　）年齢

（2）今度は、あなたがパートナーの質問に答える番です。下のFamily Treeについて、Aさんの質問に答えましょう。

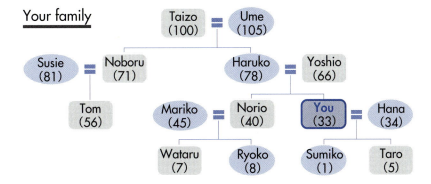

Activities Student B

Lesson 2

Student A ▶ p. 17

（1）次の写真に写っている人たちは誰なのか、パートナーの説明を聞いて日本語で写真に書き込みましょう。

（2）次の写真に写っている人たちは誰なのか、例にならってパートナーに説明しましょう。

例）The woman across from me is my big sister.

Activities Student B

Lesson 3   Student A ▶ p. 23

（1）あなたは「ハナマル・デパート　広告部」に勤務しています。鈴木ケンタさんの名刺（business card）を参考にして、あなたの名刺を作ってみましょう。住所欄にはあなたの大学の住所を書くことにします。

All Star Insurance Company
Kenta Suzuki
Sales Dept.

Minato Bldg. 1-x-x Jingumae, Shibuya-ku
Tokyo 150-0001 Japan   Phone: +81-3-9876-1234

（2）下は鈴木ケンタさんが名刺交換したときの挨拶です。これを参考にしてパートナーと名刺交換の挨拶をし、パートナーの名前、勤務先、所属部を聞き取りましょう。

Kenta

Hello. My name is Kenta Suzuki. Nice to meet you.
I work for All Star Insurance Company. I'm in the Sales Department.

名前（　　　　　　　　　）勤務先（　　　　　　　　　　　　）所属（　　　　　　　　　　）

Activities Student B

Lesson 4 Student A ▶ p. 29

(1) 下はあなたの昨日のTo Do Listです。実際にやったことには✓が付いていますが、やらなかったことについては、その理由が右側に書いてあります。Aさんが質問してきますので、この表を見ながら英語で答えましょう。

Your To Do List

☐ 髪を切りにいく	お金がなかった（no money）
☑ コンサートのチケットを予約する	
☐ コーチと連絡を取る	住所が見当たらなかった（lose / his address）
☐ 電車の定期を買う	学生証を家に置いてきた（leave / student ID card）
☑ 電話代を払う	
☑ 部屋を掃除する	
☐ 英語の宿題をする	忘れた（forget）

(2) 今度は、Aさんの昨日のTo Do Listについて、Aさんに質問してみましょう。Aさんに、実際にこれらのことをやったのかどうか、ひとつひとつ質問し、やったことには✓をつけましょう。やらなかったことについては、その理由を尋ね、表に日本語で記入しなさい。

A's To Do List

☐ talk with Grandma in Shizuoka on the phone	
☐ return the book to the library	
☐ go to the dentist	
☐ go to see Professor Tanaka	
☐ do the laundry	
☐ buy a suit for my job interviews	
☐ take out the garbage	

Activities Student B

Lesson 5　　　　　　　　　　　　　　Student A ▶ p. 35

(1) 下は地下鉄の路線図です。下線部に適切な語を入れて、B駅からCafé Rの最寄り駅までの行きかたについての会話文を完成させましょう。

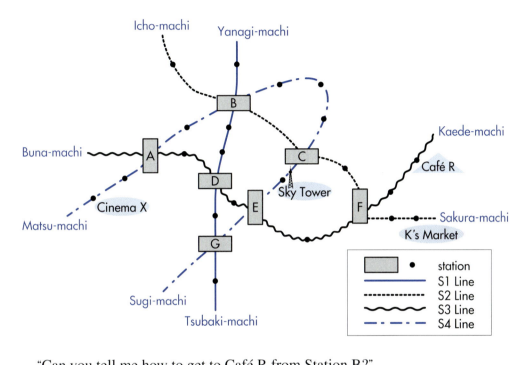

"Can you tell me how to get to Café R from Station B?"
"Sure. Take the _____ Line for Sakura-machi. Change trains at _____ . Take the _____ Line for _____ . Get off at the second stop. Café R is in front of the station."

(2) パートナーが質問してきます。上の会話文を参考にして答えましょう。

(3) 今度はあなたがパートナーに①〜③の行き方を質問し、説明に従って進んで、目的の施設を地図に書き込みましょう。
　①F駅から Studio Q　　②D駅から JJ Mall　　③C駅から South Park

Activities Student B

Student A ▶ p. 53

(1) あなたはAさんに左の商品の買い物を頼みましたが、個数を伝え忘れました。Aさんからの質問に対して、I need ...... などの表現を使って品物の個数を答えてください。

(2) 今度はあなたがAさんから買い物を頼まれましたが、数が分かりません。Aさんに質問してリストを完成させてください。How many cans of tuna do you need? で会話を始めましょう。

A's shopping list

tuna	( ) cans
eggplants	( )
rice	( ) kilos
socks	( ) pairs
batteries	( )
orange juice	( ) cartons

Activities Student B

Lesson 9

Student A ▶ p. 59

あなたはAさんと来週中に1回一緒に出かけたいと思っています。下の自分のスケジュールを見ながら相手と都合を尋ね合って、2人とも都合の良い日時の候補を3つあげなさい。

例) 質問：How about Tuesday afternoon?
    答　：I'm sorry, it's impossible. I have to ・・・・. / OK, it's possible.

Student B

August	afternoon	evening
3 Sun	Lunch with Y 1:00 p.m.	
4 Mon		Clean my room
5 Tue	Tennis	Part - time job at Star Coffee Shop
6 Wed		
7 Thu		
8 Fri		Do the laundry
9 Sat	Visit grandmother until the 10th ⟶	

Activities Student B

Lesson 10

Student A ▶ p. 65

(1) 今学期に「心理学Ⅰ」の授業を履修しようと考えているAさんは、あなたにアドバイスを求めてきます。「心理学Ⅰ」の単位を取るために必要なことをあなたに質問してきますので、次の表現を参考にして、Aさんの質問に答えてあげましょう。

　　Aさん：Do I have to <u>write many reports</u>?
　　あなた：Yes, you have to _____. / No, you don't have to _____.
　　Aさん：Thank you for your advice. Probably I <u>will</u> または <u>shouldn't</u> take the course.

Psychology Ⅰ	
You have to:	You don't have to:
・write five reports ・read a lot of books ・take a mid-term and final exam	・make a presentation

(2) 今度は役割を交代して、あなたがAさんにアドバイスを求める番です。「政治学Ⅱ」の授業についてAさんに質問し、メモを取りなさい。

```
                    Politics Ⅱ〔メモ〕
・write a report
・do research
・make a presentation
・take an exam
```

Activities Student B

Lesson 11

Student A ▶ p. 71

(1) パートナーがあなたに勉強したい言語と理由を質問します。例を参考に質問に答え、会話をしてみましょう。聞き取れないときにはCould you say that again?と言い、日本語は使わないこと！

パートナー：Now I have a question. Which language do you plan to study next?
あなた：I plan to study Hindi.
パートナー：Why do you want to study Hindi?
あなた：Because I want to eat real curry in India.

例）	あなた自身の情報	パートナーの答
言語　［Hindi］	［　　Spanish　　］	［　　　　　　　　］
国名　（India）	（　　Spain　　）	（　　　　　　　　）
目的　to eat real curry	to see a bull fight	to _____

(2) 今度は役割を交代してパートナーに質問し、上の表を埋めましょう。スペルが分からないときには、How do you spell ～?と言い、日本語は使わないこと。

著 者
森田和子（もりた　かずこ）
髙橋順子（たかはし　じゅんこ）
北本洋子（きたもと　ひろこ）

メイク・イット・シンプル
――基礎(きそ)からの実践英語(じっせんえいご)――

2015年2月20日　　第1版発行
2023年3月20日　　第22版発行

著　　者──森田和子／髙橋順子／北本洋子
発 行 者──前田俊秀
発 行 所──株式会社　三修社
　　　　　　〒150-0001 東京都渋谷区神宮前2-2-22
　　　　　　TEL 03-3405-4511　FAX 03-3405-4522
　　　　　　振替 00190-9-72758　https://www.sanshusha.co.jp
　　　　　　編集担当 三井るり子
印 刷 所──広研印刷株式会社

©2015 Printed in Japan　ISBN978-4-384-33446-3 C1082

表紙デザイン ── 越阪部ワタル（lovedesign co.）
本文イラスト ── 鹿野恵理子
準拠CD録音 ── ELEC
準拠CD制作 ── 高速録音株式会社

JCOPY〈出版者著作権管理機構 委託出版物〉
本書の無断複製は著作権法上での例外を除き禁じられています。複製される場合は、
そのつど事前に、出版者著作権管理機構（電話 03-5244-5088 FAX 03-5244-5089
e-mail: info@jcopy.or.jp）の許諾を得てください。

教科書準拠CD発売
本書の準拠CDをご希望の方は弊社までお問い合わせください。